Feminine Beauty
As Displayed by
Daughters of the King

by

Evelyn Miller

Copyright © 2016 Biblical Mennonite Alliance

All rights reserved

The Publication Board of
Biblical Mennonite Alliance
2016

www.biblicalmennonite.com

ISBN: 978-0-9982264-0-8

Printed in the United States of America

In these pages, we find the vision and conviction of a Christian lady. It is written to and for her Christian sisters. We believe Christian brothers will also find it interesting, informative and helpful. The support, counsel and leadership of our brothers will encourage our sisters to reflect true beauty and modesty as princesses of their King!

All scriptures are quoted from the King James Version unless otherwise noted.

Contents

Foreword 3

Acknowledgments 5

Introduction 7

1. A Culture Refashioned 13

2. No Sin, No Shame 18

3. Miss America or God's Beauty Queens? 20

4. Modesty Lost 23

5. Feminism's Spiritual Effects 49

6. The Contribution of Swimwear 57

7. Where Does the King's Daughter Get Her Cues? 63

8. The Woman's Head Covering 80

9. Two Distinct Genders 88

10. The Meaning and Scope of Modesty 97

11. The Virtue and Effects of Modesty 105

12. When Modesty is Missing 109

13. Practical Tips for Personal Modesty 118

Conclusion 139

Bibliography 144

Introduction to two authors cited frequently in this book:

*<u>Pastor Jeff Pollard</u> was a speaker for the Southern Baptist Youth Founders conference and a former rock musician with a few hit records in Louisiana's LeRoux. Convinced by Scripture that continuing his life in rock music was inconsistent with his new life in Christ, he left his career with LeRoux to establish New Covenant Ministries. NCM exists for the purpose of teaching the Bible and proclaiming the sovereign grace of God. Pollard is currently a pastor/elder of Providence Baptist Church in Ball, LA, and lives with his family in a small town north of Baton Rouge.

<u>David Vaughan</u> is the pastor of Liberty Christian Church, director of Liberty Leadership Institute and president of Liberty Classical School. <u>Diane Vaughan</u> is a wife, mother, writer and popular speaker at women's events nationwide. The Vaughans and their four children live in O'Fallon, Missouri.

Foreword

Too many changes are just accepted by default without considering the implications of those changes. When evaluating historical, cultural and spiritual shifts, it is crucial that we ask and answer some urgent questions. "How did we get from point A to point B?" "What are the long term implications of the shifts?" "Are the resulting changes a reflection of greater Christlikeness and faithful biblical obedience or an increased worldliness?" "Where does the trajectory of the change take us and our children?" "Are we experiencing a genuine spirituality or a camouflaged carnality?" Wisdom is required in assessing whether those shifts are positive or negative.

For the follower of Christ, the public undressing of the culture and the church cannot in any way be seen as positive. How did we get here? How has the loss of modesty contributed to the sexual distortions we see in our culture? Certainly today we are seeing the long term results of feminism and rebellion that were sown by the enemy in past generations. If one can evaluate the seeds by the tree, and the tree by the fruits, then one should certainly be able to see that the seeds of this tree have not been godly.

In this book Evelyn does us a great service by helping us to evaluate the corrupt fruit. She brings a unique and well-researched perspective on how we have gotten to the place we are today. As our sister "connects the dots" of history, culture, and spiritual influences, it becomes very clear that the root is corrupt and the fruit is rotten.

But we are not left to flounder in a sea of pessimism. Diagnosing and evaluating is only the first part in fixing a problem and reversing the wrongs. When changes take us away from biblical truth and holiness, someone must provide a clear call to Gospel-centered transformation. Intentional effort must be invested in providing biblical answers and solutions to get us back on track. We are indebted to our sister for doing just this. This book is an important part of speaking to both what is wrong and the remedy.

The Biblical Mennonite Alliance Publication Board requested that this work be undertaken. It has been a long journey and a joint effort by the Board and the author to present a well-balanced, biblically sound and practical voice. With a spirit of humility, compassion and prayer that God's Spirit will reveal truth, Sister Evelyn has spoken to us plainly. Even if the culture and the larger church seem too far gone, God desires to call out a remnant of faithful believers at this time who will embrace the biblical standard. We as an Alliance are blessed to be able to endorse this message to anyone who will listen and hear.

Todd E. Neuschwander
Moderator of the Biblical Mennonite Alliance

Acknowledgments

I wish to thank some special people who have assisted me in bringing this book to publication. First, I want to thank those who prayed for me as I labored in this project. I experienced the answers to your prayers in the many times the Lord sent insightful information in a timely manner. There were also those times when I would struggle with the information that I was learning – seeking to grasp the bigger picture – when suddenly God would "turn on the lights" and connect the dots for my understanding.

A special thanks goes to Rosalind Byler and Wes Helmuth for the enormous amount of time they have invested in the process of editing and critiquing my work. I also want to thank John Ivan Byler for much of the same. It was never a desire of mine to be a writer, so I have leaned heavily on the advice of those with greater abilities in that realm.

Thank you also to Craig and Shirley Miller for giving me *The Beauty of Modesty* by the Vaughans.

I also thank the BMA Publications Board, who kindly studied and critiqued my work. Even though I wanted so much to be finished, they realized that more issues needed to be addressed. Their encouragement and prayers have given me strength to complete the work.

I especially wish to acknowledge the contributions my own dear family has made to this publication. First and foremost, my husband Steve's encouragement and support has been monumental! He has faithfully hung in there with me, giving me counsel and perspective and helping me to think through the issues involved. A big thank you also to my daughter Cristi Glick who, although she lives far away, has been such a valuable sounding board, bringing perspective as a young wife and mother. Her artistic abilities have been put to good use in the cover details as well. Also, Patricia and Clarissa have assisted me in faithfully carrying on domestic duties so that I could spend the countless hours needed in my research and writing. Thanks goes as well to Dianna and Stewart, my youngest two, for graciously understanding when I needed quietness so I could study and meditate without distraction. Last of all, my adult sons, Clinton, Winston and Sterling have been truly supportive, encouraging me for tackling such a needed topic and to "Go for it Mom!" Without my family's support and assistance, I could never have completed this project.

Introduction

Some ladies and I were waiting to place our orders at a coffee shop in Ohio. A young man, seated on a couch nearby, observed us. After a bit he rose and walked toward us. In the conversation that followed, he said, "I am so impressed by what you are wearing and felt compelled to say something. A person can tell you are godly ladies by your appearance. There is a loveliness and beauty about your appearance that is pure and good. Your clothes are pretty and feminine, but you are not sensual, and your beauty is not shown in the wrong way. Your attire makes godliness look attractive." He had always thought of modesty as something negative or unattractive. "But," he said, "you ladies are proof that modesty can be very positive. Beauty can be shown in a right way and can draw attention to godliness."

As I pondered his words, I realized that this stranger had clearly verbalized my own beliefs and the passion of my heart for women. I believe that, when we as women dress attractively in the proper way, modesty is appreciated, people are drawn to our King, we are seen as His princesses, and our clothing speaks of our allegiance to God. May we be challenged, as daughters of the King, to set the tone for what is honorable and beautiful in demeanor and clothing. In doing this, we will inspire others to true feminine loveliness.

As women, we are daughters of Eve. She was *isha* (from man, for man), the crowning masterpiece of God's creation. You might say she was the *grand finale*. And God was very pleased! Adam, I am sure, was totally delighted with this beautiful creature that God had made just for him.

Since this was all so good, why concern ourselves with safeguards? Why not celebrate womanly beauty fully and openly?

Yes, God's design was very good, and before the fall there was no need for safeguards. Not only was no one else there to look, but more importantly, sin had not yet changed humanity's perspectives.

Your sensual beauty as a woman is a treasure to be protected. It is to be fully celebrated only in the context of a committed marriage relationship. God designed it to build and enhance the family unit. However, we now live in a world tainted by sinful (unholy) perspectives. Immodesty is an open door to the destruction of the family, which is the foundation of any civilized society. We can see that lowering the standards of modesty and gender distinction has played a significant role in the breakdown of our North American society.

God did not give us precepts and prohibitions in His Word to make life difficult for us. He gave them because He loves us and desires our best. In His wisdom, God knows what will bring the most blessing – to individuals, families and societies – and His commands are given to show us that path.

My intent is not so much to provide a list of rules for dressing modestly, as it is to raise our awareness of the issues involved, equipping us with guiding principles for our protection. This will help us from being blindsided by enemy tactics.

In our culture, there is an enemy, a rebellious spirit of the age. It is vying for our loyalty, waging war against our souls. Let us be wise in a world gone wrong.

On a more personal note, please understand that I have no animosity or disdain for any lady who has been influenced in her choices by the cultural fallout of feminism. As we examine the history of fashion, and especially as I point out the rebellious spirit of Jezebel behind feminism and how these influences have infiltrated our culture, it should be obvious that we have all been affected in one way or another. Even those who have resisted feminism's overall influence can still be susceptible to *some* manifestations of the Jezebel spirit.

Do I think that every woman whose clothing and appearance choices are different than mine possesses a Jezebel spirit? Certainly not! The meek and gentle spirit of Jesus radiates from every heart truly devoted to Him. Had I not been brought up in a minority denomination where modesty was emphasized, I almost certainly would have made the same choices as most other American Christians who have never seriously considered how God wants them to dress. So when I speak of the pervading Jezebel (or rebellious) spirit permeating our culture, it is not for the purpose of condemning anyone.

While Jezebel has many faces, the one I will seek to expose is her forward, self-displaying, immodest conduct and attitude. We will examine her pervading influence throughout the feminist movement and how it has resulted in the immodesty of today. When we apply Scripture and understand how Jezebel presents herself, we will be able to spot her influence and resist her pressure. As the realization struck me of what her influence has done to our nation and of the similarities to old time Israel, I was overcome with grief for the paganism and sins of our nation.

I am also aware that many of my dear friends and acquaintances would differ in their view of what is appropriate for a Christian lady to wear. We come from varying backgrounds, perspectives, experiences and understandings. I love them, respect them, and embrace them as friends and sisters in the Lord.

In our politically correct culture, tolerance is the banner held high above the mandates of Scripture. It is also the bludgeon used by those who are quite intolerant of any viewpoints different than their own, especially when those views are based on God's standards. Because of this, we sometimes misinterpret the meaning of true Christian charity. The balance for the Christian comes in being able to speak without apology where Scripture speaks, while at the same time extending love and grace to one another where we differ on precisely how to live out a given biblical principle.

Throughout this book you will see occasional references made to the contacts I have with women (and occasionally men) on a broad scale. This is due to more than twenty years of operating a business providing a much needed service to women who still wish to honor the Lord through dressing modestly. Consequently, this has brought me unique insights and has been instrumental in providing important perspectives for my writings.

Having been asked to share from the principles of God's Word on this topic, I am very aware of my own fallibility. I pray that my humanity or style of presentation will not be a barrier to what the Lord would have you to learn. I trust that you, like the noble Bereans, will evaluate what I share in light of Scripture. I pray I can communicate faithfully, understanding that I will one day answer to God for how I have fulfilled this responsibility.

I am also grateful to belong to a church body that invites this kind of discussion. Sadly, many groups have redefined modesty or have moved beyond this point to where one would be marginalized for mentioning these things.

For the woman who takes her cues from the world, the things I have to say will sound radical. Understanding and applying biblical concepts requires a basic commitment to the authority of Scripture, accompanied by a heart of submission to the Lordship of Jesus Christ.

To the woman who has been brought up in a church culture that stresses outward modesty, I invite you to also search your heart. It is entirely possible for someone to sit in church, modestly dressed and covered with a large veil, while still having a rebellious, self-promoting attitude.

I became aware one day of how completely the concept of modesty has vanished from much of our culture. I received a phone call from a young teenage girl who was asking questions. When I used the word "modesty," she quite innocently asked, "Modesty? What's that?"

Jeff Pollard, in Christian Modesty and the Public Undressing of America, states:

> Modesty is a controversial issue. No matter how the man of God approaches this subject, he will be judged a legalist or a libertarian by his audience. It's inescapable. Speaking against current fashion and popular trends is always difficult and costly for the man of God. Still, God has called him to a course that divinely steers him toward a head-on collision with the thinking and ways of the world.[1]

This work includes numerous and lengthy quotes from other authors, perhaps more than good taste would seem to allow. I am keenly aware of this, but as I read the writings of authors David and Diane Vaughan, and also the writings of Jeff Pollard, I was impressed with their skillful treatment on the subject of modesty, especially as it pertains to the spiritual truths surrounding the issue. Some of their comments were so very well stated that I felt I could not improve on them. I acknowledge that many of the concepts, beyond the direct quotes which I am sharing, are heavily linked with phraseology from their writings. Therefore, it is with their permission that I share some of their wisdom and insights with you. I have also leaned heavily on the insights into the history of the feminist movement as researched and compiled by author and speaker Mary Kassian in her book, *The Feminist Mistake*.

As we examine the topic of modesty and how it applies to our appearance, I invite each reader to prayerfully examine herself in light of Scripture for clearer understanding and response to the divine will. The power of the gospel enables change and growth precisely because it frees us from needing to defend our past. We can acknowledge our Lord calling us, be forgiven for our past and freely respond to Holy Spirit conviction.

We sincerely desire to encourage Christian women to embrace and live out these principles from the Word of God, even those discredited by many churches today. May our adornment be beautifully modest and draw others to admire our King!

1

A Culture Refashioned
"They Did Not Like to Retain God in Their Knowledge"

If you had visited a public school classroom in the 1950s, you likely would have seen Bibles on the students' desks as part of the daily curriculum; today its presence in the classroom, even in the personal possession of a student, is practically forbidden. Children in public schools are being censured for even mentioning God. When measured by biblical standards, the ensuing decline of morals in the United States has been continuously accelerating in recent years. Despite its earlier Christian foundations, American culture is no longer significantly impacted by the Christian religion.

Our culture and our churches have lost a proper fear of God – a fear based on respect that demands obedience. One hundred years ago, American society in general still cared about what God thought, as revealed in the Bible. That is no longer true. "There is no fear of God before their eyes."[2]

John Whitehead noted:

> The modern Christian has succumbed to secularization . . . As a consequence, [his] faith ineffectively fails even to minimally raise the ethical standards of the American population.[3]

Well known theologian R.C. Sproul says:

> I doubt if there has been a period in all of the Christian history . . . when so many Christians are so ineffectual in shaping the culture in which they live as is true right now in the United States.[4]

As Christians – imitators of Christ – we are called to be salt and light:

> You are the salt of the earth; but if the salt loses its flavor, how shall it be seasoned? It is then good for nothing but to be thrown out and trampled underfoot by men. You are the light of the world. A city that is set on a hill cannot be hidden. Nor do they light a lamp and put it under a basket, but on a lampstand, and it gives light to all who are in the house. Let your light so shine before men, that they may see your good works and glorify your Father in heaven.[5]

How do we understand these verses? In *The Beauty of Modesty*, David and Diane Vaughan explain:

> At a minimum it means that the church should not be like the world, nor be assimilated into the world, but somehow be different. More fully it means that the church should have a redemptive impact on the world. In fact, the purpose of salt is to halt corruption. Thus the church should impact the culture in such a way that the moral corruption that naturally flows from fallen human nature is hindered. The function of light, of course, is to dispel darkness . . . In a word, the church should be a unique people whose lives are radically different from the world, being transformed by the Word and Spirit of God into the moral image of Jesus Christ.[6]

Unfortunately, the salt in our land is losing its savor. Pollster George Gallup has found that church attendance has little effect on people's tendency for pilfering, cheating or lying.[7] It seems apparent that churchgoing hardly affects people's standards of modesty, either, as evidenced by a caller on a Christian radio broadcast identifying himself as a Christian in law enforcement.

The issue of modesty was the topic that day, and the officer told of how he had been trying to witness to a non-Christian co-worker. His friend was then hired as a security officer in this man's church. After working his Sunday shift as security, he lamented to his Christian friend, "I thought church would be a safe place." He was disappointed to realize that immodesty was such a problem inside of a church. He said the women in church were no different from any others, and he had to battle just as hard to maintain right thoughts as when on the street.

What does this say about modern Christianity? When the power of the gospel does not affect the lives of believers, its power and effect on unbelievers are minimized.

The feminist movement has played a very significant role, not only in the structural reshaping of the family, but also in reshaping society's view of God. In divesting God of His more masculine attributes, the church and society now see God in more feminine terms. This, along with humanistic thought and influence, has lowered our view of God. God's Name is not being hallowed. In the words of A.W. Tozer:

> The low view of God entertained almost universally among Christians is the cause of a hundred lesser evils everywhere among us . . . It is impossible to keep our moral practices sound and our inward attitudes right while our idea of God is erroneous or inadequate.[8]

What we believe about God is going to shape every area of our lives. Fashions are dictated by the attitudes and beliefs of a culture. As we see the decline of morals, the immodesty and the inattention to proper appearance around us, we realize that what we are seeing on the outside is not really the main issue. These things are only a reflection of what is going on inside. To change the outside without dealing with the underlying heart and belief issues is an incomplete solution. In the words of the Vaughans:

> When we see an immodest woman, what are we seeing? Not only a lot more flesh, but a lot more than flesh. We are seeing the incarnation of a worldview – but it is not a Christian worldview. It is a pagan one.[9]

How did it happen that our society has changed from a culture with public standards of modesty to a culture that accepts the public undress seen today, even in churches? What we are seeing today is not merely revolving cycles of fashion as has occurred over centuries. Sadly, we are living in one of the most effeminate, pornographic and sensually saturated cultures in the history of civilized peoples. Many times when great nations were brought down, clothing played a significant role in the demise. It is not difficult to understand why.

We hear concerned moral leaders of today decry the veritable decline of virtue seen through divorce, pornography and the slaughter of unborn babies. These issues have become the standard whipping points of those who bemoan the evils of our day. Of course I completely agree with these concerns, but in our attempts to remedy the moral plight of our day, can we also address the issues of immodesty and the feminist beliefs that are largely responsible for this moral decay? There is a causal virus for the symptoms of the sickness we see today, but few voices are willing to speak clearly to the issue. May God bless those who have, and may many more join in!

There are even fewer who are willing to promote and practice those visible symbols of gender distinction and submission that were customary not so long ago. There is a movement among some within Christianity to once again, in obedience to Christ and the Bible, practice the wearing of these symbols. I applaud the courage this takes – it is not fashionable today, and never will be.

In reality, following Christ has never been culturally popular. Most of the New Testament writers were killed for following Christ. In Hebrews 11 we read that our "cloud of witnesses" possessed faith, but the proof of their faith was always evidenced by obedient action – even in the face of great cultural opposition. This is because they lived with an eternal perspective, realizing that they were just strangers and pilgrims – their true home was in another country.

May that perspective be ours as well – looking to our Lord Jesus Christ and His Word for direction instead of following our culture.

> . . . But be ye transformed by the renewing of your mind, that ye may prove what is that good, and acceptable, and perfect, will of God.[10]

2

No Sin, No Shame
Sacrifice, Atonement, and Covering

The story of Creation in Genesis 1-3 identifies God as the sovereign Creator of all things, as well as the originator and designer of clothing. It is important to understand that, in the beginning, nakedness was not shameful. In fact, "God saw everything that he had made, and behold, it was very good."[11] Although Adam and Eve were naked, they felt no sense of public disgrace or humiliation; their nakedness was very good because God had created them that way. Under these circumstances, clothing was unnecessary.

What transformed good nakedness into something shameful? And why did God Himself cover man's body? Nakedness was good until Adam and Eve rebelled against God. At that point sin entered and shame followed. Now their perspectives were changed.

> And the eyes of them both were opened [including the knowledge of good and evil] and they knew that they were naked; and they sewed fig leaves together and made themselves aprons . . . and [Adam] said, I heard thy voice in the garden, and I was afraid, because I was naked; and I hid myself. . . . Unto Adam also and to his wife did the LORD God make coats of skins, and clothed them.[12]

It may be helpful to note that the word used for the coats which God made for them would indicate that they covered the body at least from the neck to the knees.

As a result of Adam and Eve's fall into sin, the first thing God addressed following the curse was the issue of appropriate clothing to cover their nakedness. The knowledge of their sin had now transformed their experience of good nakedness into stinging, humiliating shame. Blushing and disgrace entered history. Thankfully the story does not end there. In His great mercy God provided a covering.

It is interesting to note that the covering for their nakedness after they had sinned required the shedding of innocent blood, which is symbolic of the covering required for my sin and yours. They needed neither sin removal or physical covering before the fall. Once sin entered, humankind's guilt brought shame which needed to be covered by sacrifice – and to eventually be remedied by Christ's death on the cross. Likewise, our physical bodies need to be covered as a tangible reminder of God's remedy for our guilt and shame. Christian believers will, for all eternity, be clothed in white, symbolizing visually that we are covered spiritually by the righteousness of Christ.

3

Miss America or God's Beauty Queens?
Whom Does Your Life Honor?

In 1 Timothy and 1 Peter, God gives His perspective of the ideal woman. The model He presents reveals who God truly made us to be. This will provide a foundation for being the kind of woman who will be an asset to society, fulfilling the God-glorifying role He designed for His daughters. Rather than seeing these as prohibitions, may we see them as they are – a model for true *out of this world* beauty! Physical beauty fades and wrinkles with time, but godly adornment does not fade with time – it becomes ever more lovely. Let's take a moment to examine God's model.

1 Peter 3:3-5:

> Whose adorning let it not be that outward adorning of plaiting the hair, and of wearing of gold, or of putting on of apparel; but let it be the hidden man of the heart, in that which is not corruptible, even the ornament of a meek and quiet spirit, which is in the sight of God of great price. For after this manner in the old time the holy women also, who trusted in God, adorned themselves, being in subjection unto their own husbands.

Peter, by the guidance of the Holy Spirit, here gives instructions to wives concerning their relationship with their husbands. The picture given is of a woman whose heart trusts the Lord so securely that she is willing to allow the Lord to work through her husband in giving her direction and guidance. She is decorated with the beauty of a gentle and quiet spirit, which God counts as a great treasure. It is through this settled trust in the Lord, evidenced by a gentle spirit and good works, that the Spirit of Christ – His peace, radiance and beauty – exudes from her life.

1 Timothy 2:9-10 further instructs:

> . . . Women should adorn themselves in respectable apparel, with modesty and self-control, not with braided hair and gold or pearls or costly attire, but with what is proper for women who profess godliness – with good works.[13]

Here in 1 Timothy, the word "respectable" comes from the Greek *kosmios*, meaning orderly, decent and decorous. This speaks not only of the outward manifestations of dress and actions, but also of the inner life which finds expression outwardly. It starts in the heart.

Similarly, the attitudes of modesty and self-control are also evidenced in both the inward attitudes and outward bearing and appearance of a woman who embraces the heart of Jesus. These attitudes of reverence toward God and respect for oneself and others restrains a woman from presenting herself in a way that is an offense to decency. Her modesty of heart will not allow her to dress in a show-off fashion, either through excessive ornamentation or openly flaunting her sensual charms.

Modesty and self-control are the complete opposites of pride and vanity. A vain woman craves spectators who will stroke her ego, and her clothing reflects the passion of her heart – which is herself. Conversely, a godly woman desires to be a blessing to others, seeking to reflect the passion of her heart—Jesus Christ. When others see her, they see Jesus. He surrounds her like an aroma. Having been with her, they feel they have come nearer to Christ. Somehow they view her as beautiful, without even having considered why.

Feminism fails to realize that the value and loveliness of true womanhood is a joyful other-centeredness. In short, feminism is all about self-exaltation, but daughters of the King live with a passion to exalt Him! These are important principles to keep in mind as we take a tour of the history of clothing, fashion and societal shift.

4

Modesty Lost
How Did Our Culture Forfeit Its Principles?

Secular historian James Laver notes how fashion comes and goes. He says that:

- Ten years before something becomes fashionable it is considered indecent.
- One year before, it is considered daring.
- When it's "in," it is considered "chic."
- Three years later it is dowdy.
- Twenty years later it is hideous.
- Thirty years later it is amusing.[14]

And 40 or 50 years later it just may come around again. Isn't that amazing?

Do we realize that changes of style are not so much about what looks good on us, but really about grabbing more of our money? Clothing and fashion is an enormous business – $250 billion annually in the US alone. Keeping the trends constantly changing drives that market, making us discontent with what we have. The focus is not really on creating a better product; the aim is getting you to keep buying more. I am not suggesting that we pay no attention to current trends or fashion, but we need to think carefully about what motivates fashion changes.

In her book *Color Me Beautiful,* Carole Jackson encourages ladies to learn what looks good on their particular body shape –

considering their coloring and personal style – rather than acquiring the latest fad. She says that wearing a current fashion that isn't a good fit for one's *own* style doesn't really look stylish. Fashion clothing designers are not motivated with your best interests in mind, so be wise.

People's perception of what is appropriate clothing has changed greatly in society over the past 200 years. This happens because of changes in what is considered morally acceptable.

As we observe all around us what our culture and modern Christianity have accepted and now model, we need to understand how recently in history these things have become the norm. Obviously, we are glad that not *everything* is as it was 200 years ago!

Change is inevitable. We cannot lock into a period of history and think that somehow that will keep us spiritual, holy or pure. We need to examine and truly think through the issues, guided by God's Word. We also need to check our attitudes by remembering our perfect example, Jesus Christ, full of grace and truth.

Today, you and I as Christ-followers have more opportunity than did our forebears to be a witness in a culture whose candle light has gone out. As the light around us fades and increasingly gives way to the encroaching darkness, our candle shines ever brighter. We visibly proclaim, through our head covering and modest dress, that we believe Scripture to still be true and valid for today.

Do you realize what a powerfully positive statement that is? Ravi Zacharias recently said that there are five gospels: Matthew, Mark, Luke, John and you. By your appearance, you are letting the world around you know that you are marching to the beat of a different drummer and that the Word of God *is still* relevant today! I encourage you to show that difference with grace, good taste and

God-honoring feminine loveliness! You probably have no idea of the impact this has on those who observe you.

To accompany this witness, try to keep some personal notes of encouragement or gospel tracts in your purse so you are able, when the Spirit nudges, to share with others the gospel of Jesus Christ that brings life and hope. At times it may feel unfair that you as a woman need to stand out by looking different, but this can open many opportunities to share eternal life with others. The current norm for men's appearance is not as opposed to Scriptural teaching as it is for women; therefore, this is a special privilege that God has given you.

A Review of Clothing Fashions

A study of the traceable history of clothing and fashion reveals that fashion in vogue has, over the centuries, continually swung on a pendulum that oscillates between two functions: sex appeal (the lust of the flesh) and ostentation (the pride of life), with the god of this world being the motivator for both. Extreme ostentation (elaborate decoration) has been used throughout the centuries to signify rank or prestige. Followers of Jesus certainly did not participate in either excess. Today the pendulum has swung in the other direction, with dressing for sex appeal being the more prevalent of the two.

While these trends may have been typical of high fashion, they were often not what the common person wore. This is an important distinction to keep in mind as we look at history. Since disciples of Christ are called to simplicity and humility, we do not seek to emulate high society.

Understanding these historical factors will hopefully give us an appreciation of how Scripture addresses the issues of dress and appearance.

Clothing History Before Christ

Through all of the centuries before Christ, men and women both wore robe-like garments, with the distinguishing factors being trims, colors and lengths. Men wore garments to their knees, while women's robes extended to their ankles or the floor. This length distinction was practiced fairly consistently in all cultures, except for times when men also wore long robes. Women rarely wore shorter robes than men.

Similarly, men were distinguished by shorter hair (*how* short varied a lot from time to time), while women commonly had long hair. In God-fearing cultures, it was also seen as respectable for women to have their hair veiled in public.

Some in the ancient world were hugely extravagant with jewelry. Gold and precious stones were in abundant supply, and jewelry was a common way for nobility to flaunt their wealth and power through expensive beauty.

In general, the culturally elite woman's hair was elaborately arranged in rolls, plaits, waves, tight curls, etc. These were often laced with ivory, gold, pearls and diadems. For the common (non-elite) woman, it was acceptable to wear her hair long and flowing at home, but morally respectable women wore a head covering or a veil when they left home. Young girls, however, often wore their hair long, flowing and uncovered until they reached womanhood – likely around the age of puberty. My research would indicate that, through all recorded history until this past century, short cut hair was simply not an option for any respectable woman, religious or otherwise.

At this point, two items might be worth mentioning. First, these observations of historical practice were the general rule, but not universal; not all cultures held to these practices. We would not expect pagan societies to have valued decency and propriety. Second, historical practice, while informative, is not ultimately the basis for our lifestyle choices – God's Word is.

Clothing History AD

Around the time of Christ, women wore long undergarments with fitted sleeves. Over this they wore a long *dalmatic* (similar to robes worn by some clergy today). These were sometimes made with embroidery around the neck and down the front.

In the first millennium AD, the Byzantine Empire encompassed many of the lands encircling the Mediterranean Sea, especially the northern areas. This was the area in which Paul journeyed on his visits to the churches.

Byzantine dress reflected its Roman origins. The tunic was the basic garment, with a toga over top when going outside. Tunics were sometimes decorated with a vertical stripe down one side. The width of the stripe indicated the status of the wearer.

The common woman's outfit in public was usually completed by some sort of a head covering. While not true in the idol-worshiping Greek culture of the time, the more religious Jewish culture certainly observed this practice. While God's instructions for men and women in 1 Corinthians 11:1-16 did not align directly with either Greek or Jewish culture, the Apostle Paul was correct in stating that these were customary practice in the churches of God.[15]

The veils worn in the fourth to sixth centuries AD by Roman "Christian" women often indicated the status of the wearer, with wealthy women wearing long, heavily decorated veils, and common people only veiled down over the shoulders. The most familiar modern-day equivalent may be the feminine cultural attire of India. This includes a palla or shawl that is draped loosely around the body and flipped up to cover the head at appropriate times.

Times of Transition

Changes began to occur under the influence of the Emperor Constantine in the fourth century AD as the Roman styles slowly merged with those of Asian nations. The Byzantines began to wear bifurcated garments (split between the legs) on both men and women under straight-cut tunics; these were floor length for women and knee length for men. Asian women had already done this for centuries. Russian Orthodox clerical dress today gives us a good picture of the clothing of that area.

In 11th century France, tunics were still a constant, with long sleeves for women and long or short sleeves for men. Cloaks were worn over the top. The common, respectable married women wore a head covering in public.

In recorded history of civilized cultures where robes or pants were worn, it is only recently that women have not been distinguished by longer garments (to the floor or ankles) than men. This means that having the shape of one's legs visible was historically for men only.

This discussion, of course, does not relate to uncivilized cultures where lack of clothing, as well as other revolting practices which we would not wish to mimic, is the norm.

Recent Developments

The regular exposure of the calf of the female leg has only become customary in the last one hundred years of civilized mankind. So what we are now seeing is the opposite – taken to extreme – of the historical female leg concealment. Many women have completely embraced what was considered a man's prerogative.

The other area where women have assumed a man's prerogative is in the matter of short hair. Never before in history has short hair for women been an acceptable norm. There were rare exceptions, such as for prostitutes or the assumed disgrace of widowhood, but not as a respectable societal norm.

The Renaissance

With the 13th-17th centuries came the Renaissance. Through this period came a greater distinction between male and female apparel. Up until this time men's and women's clothing were somewhat similar in style, all being more cloak-like, but with differences – as previously stated – in color, trim and length to identify male and female. Along with these new Renaissance-era styles for women came the more seductive showing of form due to cutting and shaping to fit. Necklines also lowered, and functional buttons were invented.

Along with the invention of the printing press came the possibility for fashions to spread more readily. Hat making became big business. With the fantastically elaborate designs women wore, higher doorways had to be designed so women could walk through without needing to duck. Headdresses were quite a sight to behold! One lady even managed to have a bird cage enshrouded in her headdress complete with live birds. It is hard to imagine how she slept with this in her hair! Since so much work went into getting their apparatuses situated, they would leave them intact for weeks.

Up through the 1600s the religious English women were distinguished by the wearing of head coverings such as caps, hoods, or kerchiefs.

Throughout fashion history, décolletage (a low neckline) has almost always been associated with three P's – prestige, power and parties. It commonly coincided with times and events involving sensuality. Décolletage has been around for centuries in the form of evening wear or court dresses.

It is noteworthy that significant décolletage and a head covering did not exist together on the same person. The sensually dressed woman may well have worn some type of hat or fancy headdress, but it was almost never a biblical covering or veil.

European Fashions and the New World

As the Great Reformation came about in the 1600-1700s, the influence of the Catholic Church became somewhat subdued; this came to be reflected across Europe. Embracing the beliefs of the Reformation was reflected in the way Protestants dressed. Their somber clothing contrasted sharply with the extravagance of the elite within the culture and the Roman Catholic Church. Those who migrated to North America reflected these distinctions as well.

Maggie Pexton Murray explains:

> They came to America to escape religious persecution and brought with them the quaint clothing which marked them as a distinct breed . . . The Puritans and Pilgrims who are so identified with much of our early American history wore simple adaptations of costume

prevalent in the early 17th century, but modified to an extreme by its gray and black simplicity.[16]

Since the Pilgrims and many early settlers came to America for religious reasons, they naturally brought their values along with them. Their godly principles profoundly impacted the founding ideas of this new nation. Of course, not everybody that came did so for religious reasons, but the ratio of those with godly values was greater here than in their homeland. This was certainly reflected in the dress of the day.

At the first, life was hard and there was less time for the frivolities of fashion. As the colonies became settled and more affluent, women did again become somewhat more fashionable. Those who pushed westward onto new frontiers, however, had little time or energy for much more than the necessities of life.

The difficulties of life in the new world and their geographical separation from Europe were not the only reasons for simpler dress. The Quakers and German Pietists, including Dunkards, United Brethren, Mennonites and Amish, were all among those who, out of their Christian discipleship, shunned ostentation and sensual appeal and embraced modesty and simplicity of dress in varying forms.

Victorian Era Limits on Dress

Through the Victorian era, people generally wore clothes until they were worn out, even for three generations. There was not the frequent change of fashion as we see today. In 1660 a lady of Boston would have been perfectly in style wearing the dress of her grandmother who came from Europe in 1625.

In those days, worldliness or impropriety of dress was usually in the form of ostentation or extreme decoration of their clothing. The sumptuary laws of New England regulated what was acceptable in dress, limiting even the cost of a hat and the width of its facing. Hair styles, shoes, sleeve width and various sorts of finery were also regulated.

Laver states that:

> Modesty is an inhibitory impulse directed against either social or sexual forms of display. It is opposed both to the wearing of gorgeous clothes, and to the wearing of too few clothes . . . It is the enemy therefore of Swagger and Seduction . . . The 'lust of the eye and the pride of life' have always evoked the disapproval of moralists.[17]

In the early 1920s, states like Virginia and Ohio had proposed legislation that would have forbidden a woman to wear clothing that would display more than 2-3 inches of her throat and to restrict any girl over 14 from wearing "a skirt which does not reach to that part of the foot known as the instep."[18] In spite of resistance, hemlines continued to climb. The archbishop of Naples declared that a certain recent earthquake was an indication of God's wrath against the shortness of women's skirts. Legislation alone has generally not succeeded in maintaining modesty, try as it may, "The Lust of the Eye and The Pride of Life will continue to exercise their ancient sway."[19]

Victorian Era Fashion Extremes

As the perception of what was a fashionable silhouette came and went, women were encouraged to purchase the different body shapers that either "sucked it in here" or "pushed it out there." Of utmost importance for the fashionable was the wearing of the corset. It reshaped the upper body, forcing a very small waistline – the smaller the waist the better. This actually pushed the internal organs out of place and would cause a woman to faint very easily. One girls' institution required the girls to wear corsets day and night, turning a 23-inch waist into a 15-inch one. Fashion held women victim to tight lacing for centuries, and it almost had an appeal in the fact that it hurt. Fashion sometimes pushes exaggeration to a point where it becomes cruel, as with Chinese foot binding. Two current examples of this would be very high heels and very tight pants. Marie Jones later commented that, while a man's clothing is "allowed to fit his body, a woman's body is compelled to fit her dress."[20]

Farthingales became stylish in the 1600s and were soon followed by hoops and crinolines. These were wired or whalebone petticoats that gave the skirt an extremely wide circumference. They were considered quite fashionable, along with the later bustle. Imagine the difficulty this presented when trying to board a carriage or sit on a chair. With a few of these circular ladies in the same room, where was a man to be?

One account told of a hooped lady who encountered some bad luck on a very windy day. The wind caught her, picked her up and laid her down on the side. The poor lady had no traction with which to redeem her position. She went rolling until she landed up against a pole and some kind soul helped her to her feet.

Others also suffered dramatic consequences. Sometimes women aboard ship would be swept off deck and out to sea as a result of the near- parachutes that they wore. This was also the time of the open hearth, so not a few of these vain souls suffered the misfortune of having their hoops knock things over or catch on fire and cause them to be burned to death.

Women of these centuries tried to whiten their faces and use cosmetics that contained extremely dangerous ingredients such as lead. The term "cosmetics," comes from a Greek word meaning "I adorn." A curious factor involving the wearers of high fashion was that, being so cumbered with restraints, they could hardly move, bend, or do many kinds of work. Neither did they go outside much for fresh air and sunshine, so they were often sickly and frail. A symbol of wealth and status was for a man to have enough money to pay the doctor to come to the house regularly to care for his sickly wife.

Outside of high society, people could move more freely. Country folk dressed more simply.

In the late 1800s women began to revolt at what they, as women, had done to themselves. The ridiculously constricting fashions they wore were so hampering that they could not be free to move about and get healthy amounts of exercise or play any sports. People eventually realized that one's clothing should be her servant, rather than her master. As fashionable women escaped the bondage of such harmful attire, class distinctions also lessoned.

Women of the late 1800s and early 1900s also reacted against the extreme prudery of the Victorian era. Prudery refers to one who is oversensitive – extremely modest…to a fault. Such an individual takes modesty to the point of being obsessive.

Prudery, however, should not be confused with prudence. Prudence is using wisdom, discernment and good judgment about what is appropriate and what is not for a specific time and situation. Obviously, prudence would entail using carefulness and discretion in public, but when alone with your husband, good judgment would call for pleasing him!

The Introduction of Women's Trousers

The invention of women's team sports in 1866 and the invention of the bicycle in the 1880s gave rise to the need for a feminine bifurcated garment. These became known as gym bloomers or Turkish trousers. They looked like very full skirts. These were loose and baggy and gathered in around the leg just below the knee or down to the ankle. They were accompanied by long socks. This was the origin of pants on women. Although by today's standards the gym bloomers were very modest, they were considered scandalous back then. For example, in 1895 a law was enacted in Chicago forbidding bifurcated garments for women. It was considered indecent for a woman to show even the shape of her calf. If they could have seen ahead 100 years into the future, they would have fainted dead away.

In late 1600s Europe, cross-dressing (women dressing like men – or vice versa) had been considered such a serious offense that a woman could be hanged for doing so. In the early 1900s, however, women sometimes engaged in cross-dressing just for sport. They were being influenced by early feminists, who were becoming quite active. Just for fun, they would enact mock weddings with women wearing actual men's trousers because women's trousers did not exist at the time. This was done in college theatrical productions. Ironically, while the colleges allowed women cast members to play the male part, most did not allow any men to attend those productions because it was considered indecent and unfeminine for a woman to be seen in pants.

During the time of this early cross-dressing, most female cross-dressers still had their long uncut hair worn up in a bun. This was the case until the flappers came in the 1920s.

Flappers were young women who contemptuously and openly flouted their disdain for authority and challenged all that was considered decent for women. They were brash, given to smoking, swearing and drinking alcohol in defiance of the newly established prohibition laws. They also sported short skirts, low cut dresses and heavy makeup. They enjoyed provocative dancing and wild music, flirting with guys, "making out" and petting parties. They indulged in casual sex and frequented night clubs. They also defied traditional gender roles and the implications of religious commitments – obviously the total antithesis of 1 Peter 3:1-7. They were the popular set of their day, and many young girls embraced them as role models. They were assertive, independent thinkers, refusing chastity, modesty and morality. There is no mistaking the fact that this was indeed an outworking of the feminist rebellion.

Women before this time were not commonly a part of the workforce outside the home. Men filled most of those roles – from the telephone operator to the factory worker to the business secretary. Beginning in the late 1800s, and through the early 1900s, women began to join the workforce alongside men.

During the 1940s, women were needed in munitions factories. For safety around machinery they began to don men's pants. Now a new garment came to be produced – instead of "coveralls" they were called "woman-alls." Taking on these jobs was not always by their choice, but rather was necessitated because of World War II. Women would wear trousers for work, then come home and put on their dresses again so they could feel like ladies.

Through the period of the 1920s and 30s, however, women on a wider scale began wearing pants for sports. Katharine Hepburn was the first actress to publicly appear in trousers, opening the door to their eventual acceptance by the American public. It was not until the 1970s that it become socially acceptable to the point that employees of upper-class establishments such as fine restaurants or banks, etc., were finally permitted to wear them.

It took approximately 80 years from the first bold pants-wearing feminists to show themselves until it became widely acceptable for women to wear pants in our American society. What was the holdback? According to secular historians it was Deuteronomy 22:5. This was cited over and over. Even our government gave restrictions based on this passage. Imagine that!

While it was quoted often in our country in resistance to women's pants, today conservative Christians are marginalized or tagged as legalists or cultists by those within the Christian community who have imbibed the culture, all for using the very same passage!

Accelerated Changes in Fashion

In years gone by when Paris introduced a new fashion, only the wealthy who could afford it were considered in vogue. With the advent of the Industrial Revolution and the streamlining brought about by the assembly line, creating garments became much easier, and the cost of production was greatly reduced. What this meant was that now, at a reasonable cost, the general population could better afford what was introduced by the fashion industry. Before this, the upper classes had been able to maintain a certain sense of superiority by their fashionable attire. Now, with the masses and social inferiors copying the styles so quickly, the industry was driven to create the next new fashionable look in faster sequence than before.

Secular fashion commentator Langner, in his book *The Importance of Wearing Clothes,* tells how fashion designers took advantage of the fact that they knew that women would stop at nothing to be fashionable. He said that some male hat designers hated women and actually wanted to make fools of them. Just for sport, they introduced ladies' hats trimmed with dangling bunches of radishes, turnips, carrots and other vegetables; for one season they were the rage. An example from the late '50s was the sack dress, which made the wearer look as if she were pregnant. This design backfired when even young schoolgirls started wearing them. Now the men in their lives did *not* consider this humorous, because after all, what did this imply?

Langner describes secular philosopher William Hazlitt's impression of fashion:

> It is the perpetual setting up and then disowning of a certain standard of taste, elegance, and refinement, which has no other foundation or authority than that it is the prevailing distraction of the moment, which was yesterday ridiculous from its being new, and tomorrow will be odious from its being common . . . It is not anything in itself, nor the sign of anything but the folly and vanity of those who rely upon it as their greatest pride and ornament. It takes the firmest hold of weak, flimsy, and narrow minds, of those whose emptiness conceives of nothing excellent but what is thought so by others, and whose self-conceit makes them willing to confine the opinion of all excellence to themselves and those like them.[21]

The Push of Early Feminism

In the second half of the 1800s, America had begun to see the emergence of early feminists. They were partially motivated by just causes. A woman who became a widow or divorced might not be able to maintain legal guardianship of her children. A widow may possibly have been evicted from her own home. "In 1849, for instance, the Tennessee Legislature decided that women could not own property because they did not have souls."[22] Women also were not allowed to vote because of their inferior position. In the early 1900s, sadly, secular society truly did see women as second rate citizens, inferior to men; the "new woman" saw her skirt as the symbol of her inferiority. Of course the lie responsible for the injustice was the issue of female inferiority, but early feminists tied the skirt to the lie as well, which meant they needed to disassociate themselves from what they saw as the symbol of inferiority.

In many times and cultures throughout history, women truly have been seen as inferior creatures. This was also true of the Roman culture in Jesus' time.

As seen in Jesus' relationships, He was very clear about the equal value of women. He respected, communicated with and cared for women, exemplifying for Christ-followers everywhere how men should treat women. He did not, however, select them to be among his twelve disciples, because that involved role distinctions. True Christianity certainly does have a positive effect in regard to the respect and value of women.

The role played by the early feminists in women's wearing of pants is undeniable. They did not want to be hampered either by the clothes they wore or by their roles in life. They wanted freedom. They wanted to be able to live in a man's world alongside men and experience the same things allowed to men. They wanted to be able to dress like a man, live like a man, smoke like a man and vote like a man. Since the skirt was symbolic of their gender, it had to go!

In the late 1800s Mary Tillotson was outspoken in trying to encourage dress reform. In her words:

> Much of the present antipathy to [wearing of pants] by women, probably arose from the rustic adage that wives who persisted in expressing their views, or maintaining some rights, wanted to rule their husband; or as the phrase went, 'to wear the breeches' . . . Yet the

implied idea that pants are allied to power, is correct, and long, entangling skirts are as plain a type of general lack of power.[23]

The authors go on to say that:

By wearing pants, a woman outwardly associated herself with the authority exclusively held by men. In daring to be photographed while wearing trousers, these iconoclasts broke the delicate and fragile mold in which the ideal female image had been made and re-created themselves as autonomous and self-made women.[24]

The early feminists fully intended to deconstruct and blur the gender roles. They wanted women to be able to choose their own lifestyles. Some of those early feminists were lesbians and, while the theories for the causes of lesbianism may vary, history does clearly acknowledge that feminism has been the major player in the cause for lesbian appetites and lifestyles.

Lesbianism was the acid test of allegiance to the feminist cause. Since women were largely reacting to men's domination, they could now, by their dress, join men and thus shut themselves off from romantic relationships with the gender that had wounded them. Also, by dressing like men and taking on male roles, they could elevate their standing among men, thereby protecting themselves from thoughtless male chauvinism or brutal men.

Sometimes these women disguised themselves so well that their gender remained a secret for years. They wore actual men's garments because there was no such equivalent garment in a woman's wardrobe. Cross-dressing, especially when it was practiced in conjunction with short-cut hair, was considered a true indication of a desire to be a man. They wore their male attire in defiance of the expected gender roles. Adopting the clothes often also included adopting the manners of men – smoking cigarettes, drinking liquor and talking men's slang. These females were seen as "mannish" women.

Such extremes were not as true of women who wore the feminine billowy gym bloomers. These were often worn out of necessity or for convenience, not always for the same reasons as the feminists.

Cross-dressers had a variety of motives. Sometimes they desired better pay – to earn a man's wage. Other times they just wanted men to actually take them seriously, as in the case of Amelia Earhart, who wanted to compete in the world of aviation. Sometimes they were women in combat who wanted to be with their husbands or lovers – they didn't have Skype, texting or cell phones. Others just wanted to be able to go out and see the world the way a man could. Some wanted to experience adventure as did Calamity Jane in the late 1800s.

Until the mid-1800s, ladies typically pinned their long hair up into a bun and wore something on their heads to attend public occasions. Necklines were high, dresses long (to the floor) and arms covered. Ladies wore stockings when away from home. After 1910, hemlines moved up to the ankles. During the Roaring Twenties, the effects of the women's liberation movement were beginning to be seen, especially in the world of fashion. For the first time in costume history, women's legs were seen, with hemlines rising to the knees. It was about this time that women quit wearing their long hair up in a bun and, following the lead of the flappers, began cutting it short.

As though in penitence, just before the Wall Street Crash and the ensuing Great Depression which brought an end to the flapper era, the hemlines came plunging back down to mid-calf. However, the damage of this revolution had been done. With the introduction of Hollywood and television, the stage was set for the continuing demoralization of our society.

Lest we judge the women of this era too harshly, we should remember that the bloodshed of World War I had taken a huge toll on the male population in this period of our nation's history. After the war, the ratio of available young men to marriageable young women was thrown off balance. There were 5 million fewer males than females. The challenge to "catch your man" was a stiff one, and many women used their charms to aid in this pursuit.

In retrospect, one would have to conclude that the flappers had been driven by the spirit of rebellion, a Jezebel spirit, completely disregarding Scripture. They were easily recognized by their outward appearance and were the creators of what we today see as the modern woman. They redefined womanhood.

During the 1940s and '50s, societal standards continued their transformation.

Elasticized knits aided the designer or seamstress in creating the sensual look. Before these knits were available, accentuating the body beneath the clothes had to be done by skill in the bias cut or contour designing. Now the knit fabric by its very design brought out the shape of the body underneath, thanks to the elasticity and drape. This fashion look was popularized by Hollywood.

In the earliest part of the 20th century, women did not use cosmetics or even perfume. Lipstick especially was taboo for decent women because it was considered as having overt sexual connotations. As the flappers' and the entertainment industry's influence took effect, however, things such as lipstick and eye shadow became commonly acceptable. Young fans everywhere wanted to copy their favorite entertainers. Marilyn Monroe was a very influential figure in her day, changing public perceptions in regard both to nudity and the acceptability of flaunting one's sexual charms. With the rise of television, Hollywood actors became the trendsetters in all of current fashion. It is interesting to note that, though cosmetics are now widely used and no longer carry the same stigma, heavy eye shadow and lipstick are still today seen as sexual statements.

During the 1950s, while the hemlines were up to the knee, the skirts were very full and swinging, known as *poodle skirts*. These soon gave way to the more sensual body-skimming pencil skirts. The shirtwaist dress was a classic during this time and has retained its popularity more than any other dress style in American history.

The Revolution of the 60's

Prior to the 1950s, teens generally dressed similarly to their parents; but now, secular authors note, "a rebellious and different youth style was being developed."[25] Teenagers (a term first coined in 1938[26]) were the driving force behind the '50s and '60s fashion. As the cinema, TV and rock 'n' roll music swept the American culture, the youth market rushed to copy the style of the stars. After the Vietnam War, teen fashion became a huge industry, with parents becoming wealthier and teens spending more money on clothes.

By the 1960s, taboos were becoming extinct. A prevailing spirit of rebellion evolved to a whole new form. The "flower children" walked the streets with painted faces. These flower children were synonymous with hippies, who emerged toward the latter part of the decade, embracing left-wing politics and lifestyles while rejecting established culture. They advocated love and peace and explored eastern religions. The rebellion of the era further expressed itself in the indulgence of free sex and drugs. Their dress, music and attitudes all screamed of rebellion. It was a revolt against all established norms of decency and propriety.

Women's wearing of jeans became much more common at this point. As stated by Maggie Pexton Murray:

> Pants in all forms and versions became one of the uniforms of the day. Perhaps not so much because of any "unisex" drive, but because wearing pants was another expression of the rebellious spirit.[27]

Although Murray was not identified as Christian, she understood clearly the philosophical implications of women wearing pants. We as Christ-followers recognize also the prevailing spiritual forces that were in motion.

Thanks again to stars like Marilyn Monroe, lower necklines were also gaining acceptability. Physical exposure demonstrated unabashed pride in the body and symbolized sexual prowess and "girl power." A newspaper of that era described how secular men saw this. They thought it an exciting opportunity for their own enjoyment, while at the same time declaring, "But not on *my* wife!" Deep décolletage has for millennia been a part of prestige, power and parties. It is intended to excite sexual passions. This is nothing new. Today, however, it is everywhere – you can't get away from it. There is no safe place anymore.

What is truly tragic is how modern Christianity has succumbed to this societal mindset. If you doubt this, try taking your family to a modern Christian wedding. Your sons may need heavy shades! How can publicly appearing nearly topless be acceptable? Tell me, how does this promote purity and holiness? What kind of spiritual gymnastics must it take for modern clergy to make the concessions of conscience necessary to officiate at this kind of show?

As Mary Kassian states:

> Exposing the body is a mark of female pride and power. Today's young women cater to a pornographic culture. They wear less and take it off more often. And it is their personal decision to do so. Ultimately, therefore, the trend is merely an example and outworking of feminist thinking.[28]

Cultural Fallout of the Sexual Revolution

Many secular writers commenting on this era readily admit that changes in clothing fashions were a major force in helping to bring about the sexual revolution of the 1960s. This is no small admission, especially when one understands just how sweeping and devastating the effects of the sexual revolution have been. Consider with me how absolutely enormous it has been in the tearing down of faith and virtue in our day – and clothing was one of the key factors! Of course, the likes of Darwin, Freud and Kinsey helped pave the way.

If the ideas and standards requiring modesty in earlier days had not been relaxed, the sexual revolution could not have taken place as it did. Hollywood could not have a profitable market for the current rampant sexual promiscuity and degrading material it sells today.

Further consequences of the sexual revolution include a continuing increase in pornography, human trafficking, violent crimes against women, rape, child porn, pedophilia, legalized abortion and homosexuality. With the new morality, public high schools – and now even middle schools – are finding it necessary to provide daycare for the babies of students.

Women wanted freedom of lifestyle choices, but without the consequences. Birth control pills enabled musical beds and free sex. However, the promised freedom came with an unexpected price tag: STDs, single parenthood, easy divorce and broken homes with fractured families. This led to increased juvenile delinquency and substance abuse. These, in turn, are the reasons for a myriad of social woes and miseries – brought about in great part by the sexual revolution. What began for women as the promise of liberation has ended up being very damaging to women.

Is this surprising? Ideas have consequences. Our society is reaping what has been sown – payday has come! If you run an engine on the wrong kind of fuel, your vehicle won't work; it will not transport you as desired. When society ignores the Creator's instruction manual for families, it is bound for failure. God didn't give us a grid map without good reason. Ignoring His prescription for life has consequences – disastrous consequences! Our society as a whole (and worst of all, innocent children) is paying the price. I cry at the injustice; it tears at my heart!

The 70s and Beyond

In the 1970s, immodesty reached a bold, new level with the advent of the mini skirt. Welsh designer Mary Quant, the mother of the mini skirt, admitted that her intention was "to dress women so that men will feel like tearing the wrapping off." She was then asked what the point of fashion was and where it was leading, to which she replied, "Sex." [29]

Other factors have also made their impact on fashion, and then on lifestyles.

Punk rock musicians were known for their androgynous traits; they made popular the unkempt appearance of ripped jeans, torn T-shirts, scruffy hairdos, worn-and-torn looking clothes, filthy untied tennis shoes, a makeshift thrown-together look and a general impression of poverty. Ugly became cool. The bizarre and crazy exhibitions we see *on* people's heads today are but an outward manifestation of what is going on *inside* the head. They seem to get a sense of delight out of challenging decency and the norm.

Next to come were midriff exposures, body piercings and acid-washed jeans – associated with heavy metal. With this grunge look came predominantly black clothing and the wearing of chains.

The current pants-slouching-off or crotch-at-the-knee style for guys had its origin in prisons as a means of conveying the message to other guys that they were "available."

An Altered Worldview

Young people today are taught that they are merely creatures of random chance, therefore life has no real meaning. Add to that the disparaging messages in the lyrics of modern day music. In reality, today's sloppy, torn, haphazard and immodest attire is only a reflection of a distorted and pagan worldview. When you see shredded jeans, understand that it reflects what they believe about themselves and the world. These observations should not cause us to shun others or stand aloof; rather, it should motivate us with compassionate hearts to reach out to them.

As our culture has, for the most part, discarded biblical instruction as irrelevant, is it possible that the massive disrobing, piercing and tattooing we are witnessing could all be part of the progression of a pagan culture toward anarchy and a primitive society? As I was waiting at an intersection one day, a motorcyclist pulled up alongside me with the words "Pure Hate" artistically tattooed in large letters across his forearm. I can hardly imagine that many will not one day wake up to deeply regret dyeing their skin permanently.

As children of God and heirs with Christ, our bodies belong to God.

A minister/counselor recently told me that, in working with demonically oppressed people, they are seeing visible manifestations of connections between tattoos and stud piercings and demonic control. I do not pretend to understand all that is going on with these current crazes, but one thing is abundantly clear to me – body mutilating, tattooing and paganism are clearly intertwined.

Clothing on the market today, especially children's clothing, is saturated with symbols and characters associated with evil, the supernatural and the demonic. Violent movies and the music of today have also become agents of demonic infiltration and control. It seems apparent that the next generation is becoming spiritually conditioned in many ways through desensitization to and familiarity with evil.

It is easy to see the enemy's involvement in introducing the current trends and fashions. They speak of rebellion, hopelessness, disorder, lust, shamelessness, demonic bondage, distortion and confusion – all so opposite to the Christian message of freedom and the pure beauty and radiance of true modesty. Vigilance protects those within its care.

5

Feminism's Spiritual Effects
God or Goddesses?

A distortion of Scripture that came about as a result of the feminist movement was the misinterpretation (declaring merely cultural) of the first half of 1 Corinthians 11. Understanding the biblical teaching about long hair and the head covering had not been a problem for Christians for millennia, until feminism came and distorted the understanding of the passage. During this time, while Russia was persecuted and closed off under communist rule, the Russian Christians commonly understood and practiced this as well, typically wearing beautifully patterned scarves. But in the late 1980s, during the Reagan-Gorbachev years, *glasnost* came and the doors opened up to missionaries from America. Many of their church leaders – men who had spent many years in prison for the cause of Christ – became dismayed as they saw Western influences now coming into their churches and telling their people that these things are no longer necessary.

In 1991, some prominent Russian Christian leaders from Moscow, in an effort to preserve the faith of their people, drafted and signed a document pleading that American church organizations stop sending what they saw as demonic "Christian" music. They called it "music from hell." They expressed concern that it would desensitize and desecrate their teenagers. A member of the Russian Parliament, Sergei Andropov (Deputy Chairman of the Committee for Social Policies), read that letter and as a result, "Two weeks later, at the urging of the Russian Orthodox Church, the Russian Parliament passed legislation restricting Western missionaries from coming into their country".[30]

Much could be written about how the women's liberation movement has changed our society. From our vantage point it seems, however, that the blame cannot be laid entirely at the feet of these women. I am certain that there were times when men did not model Christ's love and proper leadership to their wives and daughters, which increased their susceptibility to embracing its tenets. Women are equal in value before God, a truth that chauvinism does not recognize. In spite of such possible provocation, the negative effects of women's lib on our society have been monumental!

The movement was in great measure birthed and driven by a spirit of rebellion: women declaring their independence from the shackles of the patriarchal order and disregarding the mandates of Scripture while hoping for better results. If it seems that "women's lib" is a thing of the past or some benign, mid-century movement, I would recommend for your reading the book *The Feminist Mistake*, by Mary Kassian. She brings an intelligent, historically well-documented and shockingly eye-opening insight into the roots, intentions, progression and fallout of the movement. It is a heavy but fascinating and informative read, revealing how the spirit of Jezebel (my terminology) manipulated the movement. Reading the history should clear out the confusion in our understanding of why things have gone so wrong in our families and society today. This will help to provide protection against the subtle fallacies afloat today in the culture and theology.

The feminist movement has not gone away. Its ideas and philosophies have become mainstreamed and thoroughly integrated into our society's thinking. In short, it has been the ruin of manhood and is destroying the patriarchal structure. It was intentionally masterminded to do so. Pornography (an overt form of control over men's minds) and rampant immodesty have all been part of that satanic plot, along with the movie industry frequently making men look like dunces. Although some feminists regard pornography as degrading and using women, most fail to understand that this vice is the result of their own rebellion against the biblical standard.

There has also been a deliberate distortion of the view of God. Instead of God as *He* is, the spiritual feminist leaders crafted a god more to their own liking. They have fashioned a god in their own image – a feminized god: graceful, forbearing, loving and sweet, non-authoritative, more "soft and fuzzy" – one that better suits their lifestyles.

II Timothy 4:3 tells us, "For the time will come when they will not endure sound doctrine; but after their own lusts shall they heap to themselves teachers, having itching ears." We must beware, because some of today's Christian authors and teachers have fallen prey to these deceptive ideologies. The danger here has been the damnable gospel this has produced, in which sin is acceptable and the grace of God is misrepresented. Again, this is not a random diversion; most assuredly, "the devil is in the details." Should this be surprising, considering the spirit of rebellion that birthed the feminist movement?

The changes that feminism demanded went far beyond what women wore or how they presented themselves. Underlying philosophies that have driven the feminist movement have come from both secular and religious viewpoints with both camps sharing some of the same visions and goals. Since they saw women as having second class status, they believed that women needed to break free by asserting themselves into society and taking charge of their own destiny. The feminist saw the role of homemaker and motherhood as a drag on her potential; it especially irritated her because she believed that this made her subservient to men. In 1963, American journalist Betty Friedan published *The Feminine Mystique*. Articles began appearing in women's magazines reporting a particular syndrome that was striking women. It was the "trapped housewife syndrome." All the domestic duties that a woman was expected to carry surely were beneath the dignity of her potential. How could someone "just" be a housewife and mother? It was unfair! You may have heard the term "it takes a village." This is part and parcel of feminist ideology. Achieving the goal of emancipating women required changing the structure of the family and doing away with the Judeo-Christian model. An important part of the process toward attaining that goal was minimizing sex distinctions and blurring the male and female roles.

In the early 1960s, women's lib was still seen as suspect; their ideology still was not drawing in the ordinary homemaker. She really was quite content with her role of having babies, cooking meals, baking bread, scrubbing floors and just being there to support her husband and care for their children. The leaders in this effort realized that they needed to help her understand the depth of her domestic plight! Their new tactics turned to "consciousness raising," a process through which women all over the country met together in homes, in groups of seven to ten, with a feminist leader. She would guide the discussions, exploring how women felt about their roles and carefully raising a myriad of questions about things that heretofore had been taken for granted as good and right. Does this sound familiar . . . "hath God said?" Perhaps they should assert themselves more and not let men dominate them. Should they *really* be catering to their husbands and sacrificing so much on their behalf? Why should they be the ones to play second fiddle? Also encouraged was the sharing of hurts and grievances and speaking bitterness against their husbands, fathers or other men. As they did this, they began to see how much they were "being used and taken advantage of." The goal was to get them to start questioning that which had previously been considered the expected thing to do. They were now well on the road toward the shifting of thought processes which was necessary for the acceptance of the feminist ideology.

In 1968, *The Church and the Second Sex* was published by Mary Daly. The newly enlightened woman now believed the church to be responsible for the oppression of women. The idea of a submissive wife was offensive to her. She saw it as sex discrimination that, upon marriage, a woman should need to become "Mrs. Harry Smith." The fact that a man would impregnate her and then expect her to bear, care for and nurture these children, which would make her completely dependent on him, was enslavement against her will. Since the church was against contraception, they were to blame for her plight.

To the feminist, the idea of a male, unchanging God was really disturbing. Since she did not like what Scripture taught, she believed that theology needed to change! And why even worry about all this doctrine and theology, anyway? In her eyes the mission of the church should be the improvement of the conditions of people here and now; no "pie in the sky," thank you very much! The coming of a Savior means that the purpose of the incarnation is, in effect, to aid human progress. The feminists seek for an earthly utopia, rather than the return of Christ in the clouds. They did not see playing fast and loose with Scripture as a problem at all. In their view, Scriptural revelation was still forthcoming and so truth just kept evolving and changing as needed. If dissatisfied with what the Scriptures said, they made up new rules of interpretation to make it mean whatever they wanted it to say. Their philosophy was, "Experience is key," so whatever rang true in their own experience became the basis for truth. They used biblical terminology but altered the meanings so that the language *sounded* the same, but in reality, meant something very different.

Mary Kassian explains:

> Because religious feminists do not use the same terminology as secular feminists, it may not be obvious that their beliefs are the same. But upon close examination of their definitions, it becomes apparent that the themes of feminist theology are, in fact, one with those of secular feminist philosophy. The themes of religious and secular feminism align completely.[31]

As feminism further evolved through the mid-seventies, feminist spiritual leaders turned to goddess worship; in essence the goddess was themselves. In rejecting a patriarchal God who is holy and separate, they embraced a monistic, pantheistic view of God as "all is God." This view sees God as a force embodied in all living things; hence, all matter is seen as a part of divine oneness, including women themselves embracing the goddess within, thus infusing her with power and divinity. This divine goddess status, as Kassian states, "is profoundly liberating for women, for it restores a sense of authority and power to the female body and all life processes."[32]

Feminism found a major commonality with the New Age philosophy that surfaced in the 1980s, but religious feminist leaders did not want to divorce themselves completely from Christianity. Realizing that their beliefs would appear highly suspect to the average Christian, they considered it advantageous to work within

Christianity, using slippery language to bring their views into the mainstream.

With a bit of research, it becomes obvious that the philosophical and theological tendencies of feminism closely mirror those of political progressives and modern liberal Christian and Emergent leaders. Instead of seeing God's Word as the divine map for all of life and all time, it becomes simply a tool to aid understanding. Truth then changes as *they* wish, and issues of right and wrong become obscure. Many don't wish to offend people by naming sin, so they end up offending God. God's unconditional love is offered freely, while failing to speak of the sins that are an offense to His holy character and deserving of His judgment. This robs divine love of its quintessential redeeming merits. As a result, rather than a true focus on the Christ of the cross as the only means of salvation, they believe that sinners can come into wholeness apart from the cross, through loving, healing relationships. Obviously there is a measure of truth here, which is typical of most false teachings, but it denies the work of the cross (of course they find the cross and blood offensive, too). Their "faith" really becomes about self, which is in effect creature worship. Thus it is, in reality, paganism. Romans 1 describes this path:

> For the wrath of God is revealed from heaven against all ungodliness and unrighteousness of men, who hold the truth in unrighteousness; because that which may be known of God is manifest in them; for God hath shewed it unto them . . . when they knew God, they glorified him not as God, neither were thankful; but became vain in their imaginations, and their foolish heart was darkened. Professing themselves to be wise, they became fools . . . Who changed the truth of God into a lie, and worshiped and served the creature more than the Creator, who is blessed for ever. Amen. For this cause God gave them up unto vile affections . . .[33]

Pagan witch Margot Adler, in 1985 stated, "Feminists and pagans are both coming from the same source without realizing it, and heading toward the same goal without realizing it, and the two are now beginning to interlace."[34]

Authentic Christianity and feminism are antithetical. In 1979, Naomi Goldberg, a feminist psychologist of religion, predicted that feminism would bring about the "slow execution of Christ." She said that very few within Christianity are realizing the extent of the heresy, and that this would eventually bring about the death of Christianity because it violates the very essence of the Judeo-Christian faith. Virginia Mollenkott, a theological feminist, believed that the biblical passages of Scripture that relate to women in particular were simply reflections of local customs and situations and reflected author bias or even error; since women's experiences were valid for determining truth, they had the right to judge the validity or the application of Scripture. Mollenkott also argued that Christianity needed to yield the claim that Jesus Christ is the only way to God. Mary Kassian warns that:

> Incorporating feminist thought into Christian theology may not substantially affect this generation's possessive beliefs, but it may drastically affect the entire course of generations to come.[35]

The onslaught by "Christian feminism" continues. Having substantially undermined the family and western culture, they have now expanded their efforts to include undermining the God-given biblical structure of church leadership by creating dissatisfaction within women concerning the very valuable roles which God has entrusted to them.

6

The Contribution of Swimwear
How Modesty Became Passé

Jeff Pollard, in his book *Christian Modesty and the Public Undressing of America,* lays out plainly how one facet of fashion, swimwear, has played a major role in changing the public conscience regarding modesty and acceptable attire in our society today. He draws from secular sources who openly admit what the driving forces were behind the changes that occurred.

Two hundred years ago, our society did not permit men and women to swim together. Swimming was out of the question for women, because what was acceptable to wear did not allow them to move well in the water. In fact, with their heavy woolen dresses, long sleeves and stockings, swimming was downright dangerous.

By the late 1800s, however, it became acceptable for men and women to frolic or play together in the water, prompting the need for a new garment to allow women to move safely in water. For a while swimsuit designers tried to create suits that actually covered, but the fabrics and designs were bulky and did not function well in the water. The old-fashioned standards for modesty needed to be lowered in order to meet the demand for functionality. This created a conflict, because decency demanded coverage at the same time that functionality called for abbreviation.

Pollard explains:

What was taking place on the beach was the beginning in modern times of the violent clash between the *Holy God* as the designer of clothes and *sinful men* as the designer of clothes. Fashion designers did not view swimwear as simply functional garments with a specific use like overalls. They envisioned their creations as highly *fashionable* garments, and therefore designed them both to *reveal* and *arouse*. What they clearly understood is that this new aquatic garment was merely a *symbol* of dress. This is why swimwear ultimately evolved into a form of nakedness thinly disguised as dress. Moreover, they were aware that they were undressing the American public and constantly challenged the legal limits of public nakedness.[36]

In this process, swimwear designers began forming a garment that would make underwear become outerwear. This was, of course, a problem to the conscience of most Americans, who still had higher standards of decency. However, a shift in thought occurred here, and a double standard was accepted: "It may not be acceptable on the street, but at the beach it's recreation!" Thus nakedness became justifiable, but not in God's eyes.

We see the same double standard at today's modern church weddings. Most women would never dress that way at a regular worship service, but at a wedding, it is apparently acceptable to show up at the church semi-exposed while at the center of attention. It's hard to believe – how have we come to this?

Pollard explains that, although not all were Christians, our culture's view of modesty did stem from biblical understandings. With time, resistance to public nudity slowly caved in to pressure from the secular media and the world of fashion, drowning out the voice of God's Word.

> No one held a gun to America's head and said, "Strip or die!" The fashion industry simply said, "This is what the fashionable wear" and our culture eagerly disrobed.[37]

The swimsuit now could publicly showcase the body in ways previously unthinkable. "As a people, we shifted from the biblical view of covering the body to an exhibitionist view of showing off the body."[38]

In the early 1900s, bathing suits exposed the arms for the first time, followed by a whole volley of transformation in thought and acceptability. Soon, the primary purpose of the bathing suit was no longer covering, but rather framing the body. Showing off its charms became the main event. One designer, Fred Cole, had the vision of a swimsuit that was, "not so much a garment to swim in, but something to look beautiful in."[39] With the swimsuit, his intent was to "transform the body into a living theater."[40] He created, in his words, "a dizzying vision of sexuality."[41]

Jeff Pollard further quotes Lencek and Bosker:

> Carol Schnurer, a plump and benign woman with graying hair and steel-rimmed glasses, "dedicated her life to persuading other women to take off as many clothes in public as possible." In 1931, she designed, "the forerunner of the two-piece suit. Her own showroom models were so horrified by the unprecedented exposure of bare midriff that they refused to put it on."[42]
>
> A two-piece suit first appeared in 1935 on the pages of fashion magazines. This bared a few inches of flesh between its two parts. Though some wore this daring item, it would not really become fashionable until the 1940s . . . [Newly designed] elasticated knits accentuated the curves of the body in a way that was previously impossible. Now the body underneath could be amply exposed, emphasized, and exploited in breathtakingly skintight costumes, while its designers could declare that it was "covered."[43].

Langner comments that this sort of clothing, "like hypocrites, pretends to conceal the wearer but fails successfully."[44]

Pollard continues:

> And with each new fashion season, the creators of swimwear shifted and manipulated the new fabrics to unveil yet another part of the body. Their garments virtually shouted at onlookers, "Look here! Now look there!"[45]
>
> During this period when swimming attire focused on the body's curves, men with cameras focused on them too. Models smiled and bared themselves for the media, their bodies adorning virtually every kind of advertisement. Young sirens in bathing suits became a standard item for American merchandising which marketed everything from automobiles to political campaigns.[46]

Sex sells! Why do you think they put nearly naked women in golfing, automotive and all kinds of male magazines? It has nothing to do with the magazine theme, but more men will buy the magazines, guaranteed! Godly men, however, will steer clear of such magazines.

As a frame enhances a picture, swimwear is designed to enhance the body's erotic appeal.

As we have seen, society at first revolted, but slowly those things that were once publicly decried became normalized and accepted. "Sixty years ago, dressing this way was called 'indecent exposure.'"[47] Today many pastors and teachers condone and defend these things, while anybody who dares to speak out gets labeled as a legalist.

Sexual images are everywhere. Even freeway advertisements these days have images that years ago would have been found in magazines kept for sale behind the counter to be safely snuck out in a brown paper bag.

This point in time finds me up high looking out across downtown "Sin City, USA." It is obvious that at least two dominant spirits control the city, namely Lust and Greed. Gambling is everywhere, and immorality offers its lure openly. Las Vegas is good at showing the glitzy, sparkly side of sin. When surrounded by sin long enough, it will tend to wear on you. You can get used to the darkness. When in a brightly lit room and the lights go out, you can hardly see a thing; it looks very dark at first. Just give the darkness a little more time, and your eyesight begins to adjust. It doesn't seem quite as dark anymore. What looked like black before has now become shades of gray. Eventually your conscience could become warped into thinking "it's not so dark after all." Our awareness of God's holy standard becomes clouded by our earthly field of vision.

The introduction of Hollywood and television, which emerged together, were two of the factors that weighed in heavily on changing the conservative notions of our society, as well as the church in America. Hollywood and television profited financially from one another's efforts. Whatever was concocted by Hollywood could be instantly transported into homes all over the country on the silver screen. As Hollywood barraged the American public with increasingly seductive images, what formerly seemed daring and unacceptable began to lose its shock as it was viewed again and again. People became accustomed to the sight of indecency. Can we allow the world of Hollywood, fashion and other God-haters into our living rooms and somehow think that we can maintain purity and holiness? And let us remember, conscience did not adjust overnight. It was a slow process that took lots of time.

1 Peter 1:13-16 helps us know how to maintain purity:

> Wherefore gird up the loins of your mind, be sober, and hope to the end for the grace that is to be brought unto you at the revelation of Jesus Christ; As obedient children, not fashioning yourselves according to the former lusts in your ignorance: But as he which hath called you

is holy, so be ye holy in all manner of conversation [conduct]; Because it is written, Be ye holy; for I am holy.

As disciples of Christ, to be holy does not mean that we are called to become sectarian isolationists. Jesus provided us an example when He walked among men. He engaged those who were not like Him, those who were unholy, the defiled and the outcast, offering to them the water of life. He, as the true Light, shone into their darkness in a redeeming way that spoke to their need and brought truth and life into that darkness. His godliness was not marred, except in the eyes of the religious elite, as He moved among them.

As Christ followers, our calling is to care for and disciple people – not isolating ourselves, but engaging the culture. But as we do this, we must *keep* having our hearts washed with the pure water of the Word so that what flows out of us is indeed life. If what we are learning causes us to feel aloof from others, then we have unholy issues in our own hearts. Understanding the wrongs that have influenced our culture should motivate us to a greater compassion than ever before; a loving compassion that embraces the needs around us.

Our discussion so far of culture, fashion, feminism and the development of immodest attire is but a sordid background for our more wholesome and positive study of the holy standards that our loving God has provided for human life. Let us now turn our attention to the Scriptures and God's good directives for us.

7

Where Does the King's Daughter Get Her Cues?
Biblical Principles That Guide the Christian Life

Throughout Scripture we find overarching and guiding truths recognized as principles for life. These apply to all of life. Let's consider how several of these relate to the topic of modesty for Christians.

Principle #1: The Lordship of Christ Governs Every Aspect of Christian Life

Why does it matter how we dress? Doesn't God look on the heart? Isn't this emphasis on modesty merely a lot of legalism? Certainly we have heard all these objections. Could it be, however, that those who deny that clothing is a valid issue for Christians may be missing some basic theological truths? The Vaughans, in their book *The Beauty of Modesty,* point out that the commonly held concept of what it means to be a Christian is inadequate.

> Indeed, much that is wrong with the church is partly a result of misunderstanding the real nature of the Christian life. While we say that a Christian is someone who "accepts Christ into his heart," or one who "believes in Jesus as Savior," it is striking how seldom such phraseology occurs in the Bible itself. In fact, the characteristic word in the New Testament for a believer in Christ is not "Christian," but the Greek word *mathetes*, which means "disciple." It is used 260 times in

the Gospels and Acts alone. So, whereas we say, "I am a Christian," they would have said, "I am a disciple of Christ." The difference is momentous . . . A true disciple of Christ is a learner or student. As Christ himself said, to be a disciple means to learn specifically of Him . . . "Take My yoke upon you and learn from me . . ."[48]

For a woman in our society, being a disciple of Christ requires serious commitment. The seduction to compromise is strong. The pressure to be cool, hip, sexy and hot is on.

> "The world is trying to mold her into its erotic image, to make her sexy, not spiritual. And to resist this pressure requires total consecration. Halfhearted soldiers don't win military wars. And halfhearted Christians don't win spiritual wars."[49]

Romans 12:1-2 calls us to a life of consecration:

> I beseech you therefore, brethren, by the mercies of God, that you present your bodies a living sacrifice, holy, acceptable to God, which is your reasonable service. And do not be conformed to this world, but be transformed by the renewing of your mind, that you may prove what is that good and acceptable and perfect will of God."

Vaughan explains:

> This is a call to full and absolute surrender to the will of God. We are to present "our bodies," that is, our entire selves, to God in order to live in a manner that is pleasing to Him. Using the imagery of the Old Testament sacrifices, we are bid to come and lay ourselves on God's altar and there to die to the world and to self. But we don't just die; we are to be *living* sacrifices, which means we are to live totally dedicated to God. This is no halfway measure. The animal sacrifices were not wounded; they were killed. And if we wish to please God with our lives, we must determine to fully surrender all to Him. But what God is really after is our hearts, for if He has that, He has all that we are. If we are

His, then our bodies are His. And if our bodies are His, then our clothes are His.[50]

Jesus said, "Whoever of you does not forsake all that he has cannot be My disciple."[51]

> These are tough words from a tender Savior. But there is no way to sugarcoat the message of genuine Christian discipleship . . . Christ will not play second fiddle to other lovers. He calls us to a relationship with Him that demands total surrender and total allegiance."[52]

For the woman who follows Christ, this allegiance means she lays aside her desires to be noticed, applauded and admired. She takes up her cross and gazes toward him. As she does, she turns the attention of others toward him as well.

This radical commitment to Christ will affect every area of our lives – how we spend our time and money, what we read, how we entertain ourselves and the decisions we make in selecting our clothing. It is a practical expression of his sanctifying work in our lives. Does this mean we all dress alike or in yesterday's fashion? No. Instead, we look to the Word of God to speak to the issues of our clothing instead of allowing the world to mold us into its image.

> It is a holy God who walks in our midst. We must be holy for Him. And our holiness will be reflected in how we worship, how we pray, how we serve, and even in how we dress. In the presence of the Holy, we cover ourselves."[53]

It does seem that our innate recognition of the need for clothes is connected to the awareness of our sinfulness. Could this be the reason that when tribal peoples embrace the gospel, they often instinctively start wearing clothes? Again as the Vaughans point out, the undress we see today is the incarnation of a pagan worldview.

The Question of Legalism

What does it mean to say that Christ is our Lord? Much, to be sure. All of life is to be under his divine control. His Lordship rules us entirely – spirit, soul and body. Our obedience to him is an expression and proof of our faith in him. Jesus said, **"If ye love me, keep my commandments."**[54]

Some current theological trends in the modern church have weakened the sense of submission to the authority of Christ. One is Antinomianism, which is the rejection of God as lawgiver. Another is Gnosticism, believing that God is not concerned with physical things and that Christ's lordship over us only speaks to spiritual matters.

The question of legalism or license is more correctly understood in the question "Is man the lawgiver, or is God?" Once we accept God as lawgiver, we can then apply ourselves to searching his Word to discern the many ways that he speaks to these issues.

Val Yoder speaks of seeing God's laws as a tool enabling our lives to reflect the beauty of His holiness:

> The absence of sin is the presence of beauty. Holiness is beautiful. The Garden, with its sublime ecstasy, was mankind's rhapsodic encounter with unblemished beauty. Language struggles to articulate the otherworldliness of such an environment, yet it was experienced on earth by our first parents. When sin tragically marred that holy beauty, God sent Moses to Mt. Sinai to receive His law. Here again, the unenlightened see the law as mere legalism. It is perceived as harsh, frowning, darkly complected and authoritarian. Holiness might be assumed by some to be a corollary to the law, but to see the law as beautiful would be a stretch for most theologians today. It wasn't a stretch for David! Psalm 119 gives a perspective about the beauty of the law that few write about in our time. God's primary purpose for the law was to create in Israel a beauty of culture that would captivate

the nations around them. Moses told them, "*Observe them (laws and decrees) carefully, for this will show your wisdom and understanding to the nations, who will hear about all these decrees and say, 'Surely this great nation is a wise and understanding people.' What other nation is so great as to have their gods near them the way the LORD our God is near us whenever we pray to him? And what other nation is so great as to have such righteous decrees and laws as this body of laws I am setting before you today?*" (Deuteronomy 4:6-8, NIV) The design of the law was to create a beautiful, captivating culture. The holiness of the law would cause the youth to retain their virginity, the populace to eat nutritious foods, the residents to welcome strangers, the people to be healthy, the builders to create safe homes and much, much more. The purpose involved the beauty of holiness. This environment was intended to give the world a taste of the beauty of holiness, the beauty of the original Garden . . . Jesus came to reveal the beauty of holiness through a kingdom of people that are called out of the world's system. The purpose of the church today is to again demonstrate the beauty of holiness to a world so full of ugliness. It is a very thin veneer of glitz that covers the awful brokenness of our fallen cultures today. Pain, anger, bitterness, vengefulness, hopelessness, suicide, murder, and drunkenness saturate the interior regions of culture and individual lives. The bubble of synthetic beauty pops to unveil the wretchedness within. When holiness is absent, beauty is but a mirage. The grave reality is penned by the writer of Hebrews, "*without holiness no one will see the Lord.*"

This is our calling! This is our privilege! This is our opportunity! As Spirit-filled disciples of the Lord Jesus Christ we have the honor of pointing the lost toward the beauty of holiness, the beauty of Eden, the beauty of God! The first Adam failed. The Children of Israel failed. But, Jesus will not fail. He will show the world the beauty of holiness. He wants to show it through you![55]

Principle #2: Your Body Belongs to Christ

The old cliché goes, "All that really matters is the heart." Has Christ purchased only your heart and not your body? His blood purchased you – spirit, soul and body – and he now dwells within you. You are His temple. Does he have the rights over His temple or do you? **"Do you not know that your body is the temple of the Holy Spirit who is in you, whom you have from God, and you are not your own? For you were bought at a price; therefore glorify God in your body and in your spirit, which are God's."**[56] Since Christ is Lord of our bodies, we should seek His direction on how we can please Him in the use, care and adornment of our bodies. In other words, check the owner's manual!

> What we do with our bodies, and yes, even how we clothe them, reflects our worldview, our spirituality, and our virtue . . . Christ is the Redeemer and Lord of our bodies. We do not have the authority to abuse our bodies, mutilate our bodies, or prostitute our bodies. Our bodies are not our own . . . We cannot hide behind the Gnostic claim that "in my heart I am obeying God." Oh, really? Then it should be evident in your body – in your actions, looks, words, and dress. For the soul and the body are united. As Sherman has said: "[The soul and the body] are from God; both should be for God. Man consists of body and soul; the service of man is the service of both. The body is to be sanctified as well as the soul; and, therefore, to be offered to God as well as the soul. Both are to be glorified, both are to glorify. As our Savior's divinity was manifested in his body, so should our spirituality be in ours. To give God the service of the body and not the soul, is hypocrisy; **to give God the service of the spirit and not the body, is sacrilege;** to give him neither, atheism."[57]
>
> Modesty does not demand the body be covered because it is somehow evil. It isn't . . . The body is a good creation of God; thus it is to be adorned according to His standards.
>
> But more importantly, the creation of the human body was inseparable from the creation of the human person. In other words, God did not create a disembodied soul, which for a time floated around in the air and then later was trapped in a body. Rather, body and soul were created together. This means that when we think of the human

"person," we cannot think exclusively of the "heart," as if the body is some sort of appendage not integral to the person himself. To be human means we have both a body and a soul (some prefer the word *spirit*). Or better, a human person is the *union* of both body and soul.

While it may seem as if we are belaboring the obvious, we must realize how deeply Gnostic thinking has crept into the church. It is not uncommon to hear Christians say that what really matters is "the heart." As with other clichés, this may or may not be true. If it means that God measures our actions by our intentions, then it is true. And if it means that the heart is the source of our actions, then it is true. But if it means that God doesn't really care about what we do with our bodies, then it is radically false. The Bible knows no such dichotomy between the inner and the outer person."[58]

Jeff Pollard puts it this way:

> The cry of the feminists is "It's my body, and I'll do what I want." The cry of the modern Evangelical is "It's my liberty, and I'll do what I want." Nevertheless, the declaration of Scripture is this: **"What? Know ye not that your body is the temple of the Holy Ghost *which is* in you, which ye have of God, and ye are not your own? For ye are bought with a price: therefore glorify God in your body, and in your spirit, which are God's" (I Cor. 6:19,20).** You are *not* your own, if you are a Christian. Your whole being – body and soul – is the purchased property of Jesus Christ; and the price paid for *your* body was the breaking of *His*: "This is my body, which is broken for you" (1 Corinthians 11:24; Matthew 26:26). Your body belongs to *Him*! He redeemed it with His precious blood on the cross of Calvary. We *must* consider how we adorn His blood-bought property.[59]

Principle #3: Love One Another

"Yet if your brother is grieved because of your food, you are no longer walking in love. Do not destroy with your food the one for whom Christ died."[60] If that applies to food (which is for your own consumption) then it also applies to clothing, (which is for public consumption). Have you ever thought of it that way? What goes in your mouth is obviously your business, but what you put into your brother's eye gate is also your responsibility.

> Because our clothing is for public consumption, and because it does influence other people, we must take responsibility for its effect . . . A question every woman ought to ask herself is this: If my attire were causing my brothers in Christ to sin, would I want to know? Her answer is a good barometer of her spirituality.[61]

Love restrains us from setting temptation in our brother's way. True love avoids setting stumbling blocks. What is most important to you, his conscience or your choice of clothing? If you decide your clothes matter more to you than his holy conscience, then it becomes proof of spiritual immaturity regardless of what may be coming out of your mouth. "He that loveth not his brother whom he hath seen, how can he love God whom he hath not seen?"[62]

We need to care enough about each other to "[speak] the truth in love"[63] and "consider one another in order to stir up love and good works."[64]

> We [build up] the body of Christ by instruction, admonition, and reproof. In a word, we care enough to confront. Thus, the church must mature to the point that, as a community, we are willing to both exhort and reprove others, and to receive the same from others."[65]

Radio speaker J. Mark Horst says:

> We all agree that God created men and women and gave them particular qualities, unique to each gender. We also agree that He gave prescribed guidelines for the legitimate fulfillment of sexual desire. Because of a man's physiological makeup, he responds to a different set of stimuli than women do. A man's passions are easily and quickly

aroused by sight. This is why it is so important for women, and especially godly women, to dress modestly. A woman is more influenced by touch, tender words, atmosphere, etc." [66]

Much of today's modern day "Praise and Worship" in churches includes immodestly dressed women on stage displaying themselves sensually. This is wrong! It may be called worship, but more than Creator worship is going on here – it can be a serious struggle for the man who is trying to keep his focus on God. Praise and worship of the Creator is wonderful; let us not turn it into creature worship. Our worship must be holy, for God is holy.

A plea to Christian women from a brother (from a gospel tract):

> Your brothers in Christ are not wicked, but they may be weak. And the devil does all that he can to weaken them further. They are forced to live in a world where they are continually bombarded with sights designed by the enemy of their souls to weaken their morals and destroy their purity of heart.
>
> And must Christian women help the devil do his work? Must they make themselves a temptation to their brethren, even in the congregation of God? Oh, that you could understand the fierce and bitter conflict in the souls of your brethren when you arouse their desires by the careless display of your feminine beauty. Oh, that you could hear their pleadings with God for deliverance from the power of these temptations . . . Never again would you plead for your right to dress as you please . . . A little of real love for the souls of your brethren would remove forever from your heart the desire to dress as you please."[67]

Although our liberty is real, it should never be used selfishly to hurt others. When Christian women dress provocatively, it hurts their brothers in Christ. Men are hardwired to be visually stimulated, even if they desire to avoid lust. "An immodest woman is a provocation to sin for a man. She is (knowingly or not) enticing him to lust, and should he give in, she has burdened his conscience."[68] "Garments, like all material things, are not sinful in and of themselves. But exposing or sensually packaging the body, while provoking lust in others' fallen flesh, is."[69]

The Spirit of Jezebel revisited

And why does it matter if he just gives in to the lust that tempts him? You see, the danger is far greater than just the battle it creates in his heart and mind, with guilt that follows. We ladies need to understand this. It is not a benign sin. It really does weaken him spiritually. His spiritual senses become dulled. He is not able to walk in close fellowship with God or experience the power of an anointed life and ministry while harboring this sin in his life.

I want to throw out a caution here for mothers to be careful about what is lying around the house. I remember a pastor relating how a Christian young lady came to him asking for a prayer of blessing on her occupation as a model for lingerie advertisements. He kindly told her that he cannot bless her in this endeavor. He then shared with her what he had heard from young men who had fallen into pornography. Many had told him that their introduction to pornography came through lingerie advertisements in newspapers. It served to whet their appetites for more. Her heart was truly turned toward the Lord. Taking this seriously, she realized that she could no longer, as a Christ follower, continue to model lingerie.

John Regier, founder of Caring for the Heart Ministries, was the featured speaker at a local seminar in 2013. During his address he related what they, through counseling, have found to be the spiritual hallmarks typically characterizing those involved in pornography. They include a reluctance to call things right or wrong. Truth becomes fuzzy. They will tend to view things in shades of gray. Their dulled sensitivities cause a lack of accurate spiritual discernment.

He went on to say that much of pornography comes infused with the power of demonic spirits which infiltrate and become an indwelling, ongoing part of those who have given themselves to that kind of involvement. A 2002 Barna survey revealed that millions of Christians are involved in gambling and pornography *on a regular basis!* As we let that fact sink in, we realize what is happening to the church in America.

As we draw nearer to the coming of Jesus Christ, God is once again raising up the Spirit of Elijah – a spirit of righteousness – to prepare his people for that great climactic event of history. Elijah, in his day, brought much needed warnings to a wayward and idolatrous nation. An archenemy was in pursuit of him, bent on silencing the voice of the prophet of God. That enemy was Jezebel. When he spoke prophetically, she went after him, determined to silence him. I believe that what we are seeing today in society and in modern churches is the manipulative, rebellious spirit of Jezebel. She is alive and active, obscuring truth, downplaying doctrine and deemphasizing the clear voice of God's Word concerning sin, and thereby silencing the prophets of God. She has made deadly inroads into the theological thinking of Christianity today. One of the tools of her trade is seduction through the power of immodesty. As their spiritual senses become dulled, she makes spiritual weaklings of men. They become pawns who will serve her cause; Ahabs; men who are afraid to stand up to her; men without backbone; men who won't speak for right or identify wrong; compromising men. Certain well known spiritual leaders today are afraid to call the gay lifestyle sinful. Sixty years ago they would never have capitulated, but as standards of modesty became lowered and the ensuing sexual revolution has deluged our land, it has become dangerous to speak truth. Any who dare do so may suffer retribution or find themselves in Elijah's shoes, running for cover.

In Elijah's day, Jezebel would tolerate no opposition. When Elijah's God won the victory on Mt Carmel, it infuriated Jezebel, and she pursued him with a screaming vengeance. Elijah fled for his life. Even after the dramatic display of God's power, he was struck with horrible fear, doubt and discouragement.

Fast forward now to John the Baptist, a man called by God to herald the coming of the Savior. John baptized Jesus and declared to the world that Jesus was sent from God to take away sins. He prepared the way for the Messiah by preaching repentance. He was fearless and bold, but he had stepped into Jezebel's territory. Once again the immoral Jezebel spirit reared its menacing and vengeful head through Herodias. As a result, John was thrown into prison. Still not satisfied, she would stop at nothing. She connived and manipulated and, through sensual seduction, she got her wish – the death of the voice who dared call her ways unrighteous. The granting of her wish came on a charger.

But a similarity that we see again between Elijah and John was the force of the doubt and discouragement they were struck with when threatened by the wrath of this Jezebel spirit. John was the very one who heralded the Christ and had seen it confirmed by God's Spirit descending on Jesus in the form of a dove – even hearing an audible voice of confirmation from *heaven*. At his greatest point of discouragement in prison, he needed reassurance that Jesus really was the Christ! Again, she had brought discouragement against any who dare expose her. So what can we expect today?

Where did Jezebel come from? Her name means "Baal exalts" and "unchaste." Jezebel was the daughter of Ithobaal – also known as

Ethbaal, king of the Sidonians. She was not only a Baal worshiper herself, but actively supported the promoters of Baal worship. Baal was considered a supreme god with lesser gods under him. Ashtoreth was the primary goddess – a fertility goddess. Sensuality was strongly rooted in Baal worship; part of Baal worship involved sexual acts of prostitution in their temples. The babies that this kind of worship produced at times were used as human sacrifices on the altars to appease the gods. Jezebel's spiritual contribution to the ten northern tribes of Israel under Ahab's rule led eventually to their downfall and captivity.

Do we see a correlation? America is today worshiping at the altar of sensuality. America's worship of and sacrifice to these pagan gods involves pornography, sensually graphic movies, blatant immodesty and a loose moral lifestyle with free sex, under the banner of "If it feels good, do it." God is no longer ultimate and supreme in the American consciousness. Many serve self and sensuality, which is, in essence, paganism. It is living like there is no God or as though He doesn't matter. The millions of babies that this kind of worship produces have become the human sacrifices offered on the altars of the pagan gods of sensuality at abortion clinics all over this country. God have mercy on us! The Jezebel spirit of sensuality seeks to effectively shut the mouth of the prophets of God who desire to point God's people back to God's holy standard and to worshiping only Him. Drug addiction, homes broken through divorce, crimes and the fiscal cliff we are hovering over are the beginning of the judgment of God on a nation that has left His precepts and is worshiping on these pagan altars to heathen gods.

In Revelations 2:18-29 God speaks a warning to the angel of the church at Thyatira. They had plenty of good things going on to be sure – charitable ministries and such – but Jesus said He had some things against them. They had allowed Jezebel to use her influence to cause God's servants to commit acts of sexual immorality and to partake in idolatry. They were known as the compromising church. He gives them space to repent but warns that, if they do not repent, they will be thrown, along with her, into great tribulation and her children will be killed. But to the overcomers will be given power over the nations and the morning star. This morning star depicts a visible glory that speaks of inward purity.

There are various possibilities as to whom and what "Jezebel" here may be referring, but one thing is very clear: sensuality is her ploy; it is the web with which she weaves her business. She is a manipulator and a controller, be it overt or be it subtle.

The Old Testament Jezebel had 850 prophets of Baal and Ashtoreth at her beck and call. Ahab was her puppet. She manipulated and controlled him. Read I Kings 21:25.

In our day, the Jezebel spirit still uses sensuality to seduce men's hearts and souls. Through this constant barrage of sensuality, she dulls the spiritual sensitivities of would-be godly men. Rather than standing for the truth of the Word of God, she deals in uncertainties, shades of grey, compromise and tolerance . . . all in the name of religion.

We are living today in what may be the most everywhere-around-us kind of sensuality of any civilized culture in recorded history. Certainly this is true in the quantity of available sensuality through pornography and the Hollywood media. Perhaps Noah's day or Sodom and Gomorrah may have been as bad or worse, but fire or flood have destroyed the relics of proof.

The spirit of Jezebel is clearly the spirit that birthed the feminist movement. It was without question the motivator behind the subsequent waves in the Roaring '20s and again through the 1960s to the '90s. Women rose up in opposition to the divinely appointed headship order. They were sassy, bold and committed to having it their way! The subsequent result was the disappearance of the symbols of submission to God's designed order of authority.

To be involved in the war for deliverance from this spirit, we need to first repent of the sins we have been ensnared in. Beyond that, we need to pull down the strongholds that have allowed that sin to have any hold in our lives to start with. Repentance and faith in Christ alone is what brings victory. His sacrifice and atonement are complete and sufficient for our salvation, but freedom through the cross means we also embrace our cross. We say "No" to the sinful desires of our flesh and allow the cross to put to death the old nature. As Andrew Murray states so well:

> Jesus humbled himself unto death and opened the path in which we too must walk…In death He gave up self with its natural reluctance to drink the cup . . . if it had not been for His boundless humility, counting himself as nothing except as a servant to do and suffer the will of God, He never would have died . . . humility is nothing but the disappearance of self in the vision that God is all."[70]

This death to self is a work that the imparted life of Jesus does in our hearts, but it requires our cooperation. As our flesh dies, and as his sanctifying work takes effect in our hearts, the life and nature of Christ becomes ours. That is where true victory over a Jezebel spirit lies – in Christlikeness.

An Antidote: The Spirit of Christ

When a woman has been wounded by a corrupted man in her life, she will tend to not trust men. Through her mistrust, she will tend to seek to control her life and circumstances so that she will never be hurt again. By following this path, a Jezebel spirit emerges.

The true antidote for this spirit of control is the humility of Christ. As Christ took up his cross, she may bring her hurts and lay them at the foot of the cross. As He forgave those who hurt Him, so she grants the forgiveness that Christ enables, releasing those who have wounded her and accepting that hurt as a means by which the grace of humility is imparted to her. As Christ trusted the wisdom of God, even in the hour of greatest struggle, she answers, "Not my will but thine," yielding her full confidence to a God big enough to be trusted with her security and placing her future into his care. God delights in this kind of trust, and He will do exploits in behalf of the woman who places her hope and her confidence completely in Him. This is the antidote to a Jezebel spirit as found in 1 Peter 2:23-3:4:

> [Jesus], when he was reviled, reviled not again; when he suffered, he threatened not; but committed himself to him that judgeth righteously: Who his own self bare our sins in his own body on the tree, that we, being dead to sins, should live unto righteousness: by whose stripes ye were healed. For ye were as sheep going astray; but are now returned unto the Shepherd and Bishop of your souls. Likewise, ye wives, be in subjection to your own husbands; that, if any obey not the word, they also may without the word be won by the conversation of the wives; While they behold your chaste conversation coupled with fear. Whose adorning let it not be that outward adorning of plaiting the hair, and of wearing of gold, or of putting on of apparel; But let it be the hidden man of the heart, in that which is not corruptible, even the ornament of a meek and quiet spirit, which is in the sight of God of great price.

It is a heart of submission to God and His ordained authority, and the embracing of a meek and quiet spirit that becomes her greatest defense against this spirit of control. In order to do this, however, she must be willing to fight the battle of the mind, taking every thought and action captive to the obedience of Christ, choosing to trust him at every turn and praise Him in everything that He allows. His name is "Faithful God":

> Know therefore that the LORD thy God, he is God, the faithful God, which keepeth covenant and mercy with them that love him and keep his commandments to a thousand generations;[71]

A beautiful example of this kind of trust in God is a dear young friend of mine who recently lost her husband in a drowning accident. At the graveside, I was overwhelmed with awe as I watched her after they had finished covering his grave and the crowd began singing. She raised her hand toward heaven and joined in praise to God while the tears were flowing down her face. It was a very powerful moment, depicting the highest form of worship I have ever witnessed! God takes notice when we choose to praise and trust Him with our circumstances, even in the darkest hours.

8

The Woman's Head Covering
God's Protective Design

A princess may wear a crown identifying that she is the King's daughter. Sisters, as daughters of the King we also wear an identifier that shows we belong in the royal family and are under the special protection of the King. Don't wear your "crown" as though you're ashamed of it or afraid someone might see it. Wear your crown with beauty! Wear it with honor!

Several centuries ago John Calvin made the prediction that the shedding of the woman's head covering would bring about the exposure of her breasts. This was in part prophetic, but it was also observable even in his time. The wearing of the head covering and public exposure of the breast have not in the past – or in our time – ever gone together. In centuries past when the head was covered, with a cap or veil, as opposed to a headdress, the breasts were covered as well. When the breasts were uncovered, the head was as well.

For nineteen hundred years the woman's head covering had been understood and practiced by the Christian church. Though the ways it was practiced differed, it was broadly expected for public worship. In the early-to-mid 1900s in most mainline denominations, it was still expected that a woman should wear something on her head for public worship. It was so important to them that, if they didn't realize beforehand that it was missing, they would try to find something – a hat, a hanky, anything – so that they were not uncovered for worship . . . it was that important! Mary Kassian points out that, in the attempt to deal with the inconvenient Scriptural passages addressing women per se, religious feminists such as Virginia Mollenkott chose to relegate instruction in those matters to being merely "bygone cultural customs" of certain locales and inapplicable to our day. In Mollenkott's view, since feminism's influence has shed its "light," freedom from old trappings has come, and with it now dawns a new day.

Statistics show that, very soon after wearing a head covering became rare, the divorce rate in our country skyrocketed, reaching totally unprecedented levels! To this day, divorce is quite rare in homes where a woman wears a veil. Could this be "because of the angels" – those attending spirits of God called to protect a veiled woman and her marriage? As a society, we have seen the disintegration of the home as never before. Though there are other factors involved, neither society nor the church can walk away from God's instructions without consequences.

Calvin must have understood something about the principle and the connection between the two. His prediction gives us pause and is a matter for reflection. Why is it that the diminishing or the laying aside of the veiling and exposure of the body are often seen together? Carolyn Myer, in *Know Why You Are Veiled*, observes:

> When a woman rejects the veil, saying she was in bondage, it so very often soon appears that she has moved into bondage to immodest worldly fashions. That's not true of everyone who stops wearing a veil, but it happens very often.[72]

In South Carolina, a young Mennonite man was attending a Christian college where the professor was teaching the students how to understand the Bible accurately, using the proper principles of hermeneutics. Beginning in the gospels, they worked their way through the New Testament, eventually coming to 1 Corinthians 11. The young student eagerly anticipated hearing the professor teach this passage true to the text. As the class opened, the professor said, "According to the way that I have taught you to interpret Scripture, (with proper hermeneutics) the only correct conclusion we could possibly come to on this passage, is that it is talking here about a woman wearing a piece of cloth on her head. Since that's not what we believe [meaning, how we do it], we will skip chapter 11 and go on to chapter 12." Stunned, a girl in the class asked, "What did you just say?" So he repeated it.[73] At least the professor's intellectual honesty did not allow him to teach inaccurately.

One local non-Mennonite pastor, who also served as a city chaplain, kept a supply of veilings on hand for the times he needed to work with demonically troubled women. He had come to realize the power provided for a woman who wears that "piece of cloth" on her head. The demons had obviously recognized it as well and had verbally registered their hatred for it, demanding that it be removed. I guess the demons had not heard that it was just cultural back in Corinth – that it bears no relevance in our day – or that only the principle matters. If demons have such a response to the veiling even today, then there *must be* a reason.

Consider with me; what does the veil symbolize? And what is Satan's agenda? Humility and submission are in serious conflict with rebellion and control. Might a desire to live before God in humility and submission provide a compelling incentive for a daughter of the King to be veiled?

You have likely also heard the objection that the veiling can become an idol (as a reason to not wear it). Here is a question to consider. What good thing cannot become an idol? Your husband, your children or your home could become idols as well. In fact, let's flip that charge around – what about the idols of fitting in, or approval and acceptance by others (putting culture before Scripture). Anything you worship more than Jesus is an idol. With this in mind, it is difficult to see the veiling becoming an idol, since it is worn in obedience to Christ. Nor would we use the "idol defense" against obedience to other commands of our Lord.

I have also had a number of non-Mennonite ladies share with me about God leading them, through their own study of Scripture, to the wearing of the head veiling. These dear ladies sometimes experience great struggle. They feel very alone and are frequently marginalized – especially by others in their churches. It is so different from the spirit of this age. Certain types of women – who unwittingly have adopted a Jezebel spirit – will in fact reveal their colors rather quickly through their in-your-face kind of opposition to these women who are simply trying to walk in obedience to the Lord. Standing alone is not easy.

Ladies, may the Lord bless you in your obedience to His Word! It is not easy to swim upstream. It never has been easy to take up the cross – dying to our natural desires, identifying with Christ and running counter-culture. But take courage! It is always right to be true to the Word of God, and God will bless you for it. You may not see or understand all the ways that blessing and protection will be with you now, or even in your generation, but rest assured the Lord blesses obedience.

You might know people who have been covered but have not lived true to the principle of submission. Who wouldn't see the inconsistency evidenced by a plainly dressed, veiled woman displaying a disrespectful or controlling spirit? Unfortunately, it does happen. But does the truth of the Word of God rise or fall based on the actions of people? "Let God be true, but every man a liar."[74]

It is not my intention or desire to be critical of ladies who are unveiled or who wear pants. I am grateful to see any woman who dresses modestly, loves, honors and respects her husband and has a gentle, quiet spirit. We do not judge others; our purpose is simply to encourage faithfulness to what we know Scripture teaches. We need this kind of encouragement in our day because most others in the Christian world would try to persuade otherwise.

It may be helpful to note that we are not trying to be different merely for the sake of being distinct. As our society has departed from an adherence to biblical precepts and admonitions, those who still believe that Scriptural instructions should dictate our choices in outward appearance will, by necessity, stand out. Since the Amish are widely known for their distinctive dress, wearing a skirt or a veiling of any kind may very possibly result in questions about being Amish. A relative of mine was eating with her husband at a local restaurant while rain was pouring down outside. A kind-hearted soul approached them with concern about how their horse was faring out in the deluge. Obviously misapplied labels will occur.

Years ago, plainly dressed women in society did not stand out as an oddity. Walter Beachy tells how a banker friend recalled hearing his mother say that, back in the late 1800s, an Amish lady and a Methodist lady would have been virtually indistinguishable when seen from across the street. Their appearance would have been very similar.

Is Modest Dress a Hindrance to the Gospel?

This leads to a question worth considering: Does appearing so noticeably different from those we wish to draw to faith in Christ create a barrier to the gospel? Don't we need to minimize our obvious differences from the culture around us so that we can effectively witness?

As the influences of feminism have changed what once were the preferred norms, our society has moved far away from adherence to a biblical standard (taking many Christians along). So I would raise the question – how does our becoming one with worldly or unbiblical societal dress standards help to bring our society back to the truth of God's Word – especially as it relates to appearance, family values or even the gospel itself? Do we need to compromise and pollute the water in order to bring them to the transforming fountain of life? We have seen how feminism is largely responsible for today's immodest departure from godliness. Do we now also need to bow to its influence in order to show the world a better way? We need to be willing to become "all things to all people," in order to win them as Paul did, but do we accomplish that through disobedience to God's Word? Let's look into Scripture for the principles that guide in a situation such as this.

Daniel was one who, although he lived in a foreign land, had "purposed in his heart that he would not defile himself with the portion of the king's meat, nor with the wine which he drank: therefore he requested of the prince of the eunuchs that he might not defile himself."[75] Daniel could have thought, "You know, what does it really matter? I'm away from home, my church or my relatives wouldn't see me do this anyway, so I wouldn't be offending their consciences. Besides that, if I request these special favors in lieu of the norm, the officers of the court might take me as displaying a "holier than thou" attitude and I could end up ruining any chance for effectively speaking into their lives, because I'll be marginalized as irrelevant! What's a little wine if it means I can have an ear with those who really could benefit from my biblical perspective? I know God loves me, and my relationship with Him is not dependent on what goes into my mouth anyway, so I feel that, given the factors and culture involved here, it's best to just go ahead and eat the king's food along with the rest of them." Had Daniel sought to be relevant, conforming to his culture, we may very well never have heard about him. As a result of Daniel's obedience and the obedience of his three friends, it goes on to say that "God gave them knowledge and skill in all learning and wisdom and Daniel had understanding in all visions and dreams." Scripture also declares that "an excellent spirit was in him." Would we know about Daniel hearing from God in the interpretation of the king's dreams if he had not chosen the path of obedience? Would he have influenced kings Nebuchadnezzar, Darius and Cyrus toward reverence for God and great respect for himself?

Hearing God's Holy Spirit is sharpened through obedience to His commands. When we neglect obedience to the truth that God has set before us, we put ourselves in the dangerous position of quenching His Spirit in our lives, making it more difficult to hear what He is saying to us. God only leads us further as we obey what He has already told us.

What about Daniel's resolve to keep praying three times a day in front of the open window facing toward Jerusalem? Would it have mattered if he had just shut the window or closed the curtain? It is true that God could have heard his prayer at any time or in any place, but we would not have the faith-building account of Daniel in the lion's den if he had made some adjustments under pressure.

Recall also his three friends, Shadrach, Meshach and Abednego, who stood, despite tremendous pressure to conform and do what everybody else was doing. Surely a brief bow would not matter – what really matters is the heart (so we are told)! Nothing they could possibly do could make God stop loving them – His love for them was not conditioned on their actions. God would know that in their hearts they were not really bowing, but were still true to Him.

But no! That's not how the story reads; it's not true of God's ways. Many are the subtle lies we hear today, but the Bible says, "If we deny Him, he also will deny us." [76] And still today, "the eyes of the LORD run to and fro throughout the whole earth, to shew himself strong in the behalf of them whose heart is perfect towards him."[77] This requires a willingness on our part to pay the price of obedience at any cost – even when that obedience looks terribly uncool. True faith is still, in our day as it was back then, evidenced by obedience. And when we obey, God is glorified.

9

Two Distinct Genders
The Problem of Androgyny

Our female personhood, in the way that God designed us, is a crucial part of His plan to show to the world both the wisdom of His ordained order and how Jesus Christ and His bride, the Church, relate together. John Piper, in an address to women at True Woman 2008, said:

> Womanhood is a distinctive calling of God to display the glory of His Son in ways that would not be displayed if there were no womanhood, so that our maleness and femaleness would display more fully the glory of His Son in relationship to His blood-bought bride.

As Nancy Leigh DeMoss puts it:

> The fact that God created male and female different from one another is foundational to God's whole eternal plan. When we blur those distinctions in the way that we look, conduct ourselves in our functions and in our clothing styles and go in the direction of a unisex society, we have done incredible damage to the cause of the gospel and the cause of Christ in our world. When you have patriarchal societies that recognize the leadership and headship of men, in those cultures the clothes of men and women are vastly different. When societies become matriarchal, where women are more dominant, you find that the clothes worn by the two sexes become more and more alike. As women become more masculine in their appearance, men become more feminine in their behavior – and women come to "wear the pants" in more ways than one.[78]

Deuteronomy 22:5 states:

> The woman shall not wear that which pertaineth unto a man, neither shall a man put on a woman's garment. For all that do so are abomination unto the Lord thy God.

Why would God call this an abomination?

In a postlude to Langner's writings, secular author and designer Julian Robinson states, "For almost the whole of recorded history, up until the 1960s, no effort was spared to make the clothes of the two sexes as different as possible."[79]

Robinson goes on to explain that the acceptance of unisex clothing aided in the advance of women's liberation by making it easier for women to work alongside men and perform many of the same occupations as men. This served to help bring about the reversal of roles in the home. This, in turn, contributed to gender confusion in children, which is fuel for the gay movement.

Seeing the damage to our society, Robinson admits that hindsight now understands why the moralists were so outraged and disturbed by the unisex trends of the '60s. (These moralists were being guided by the warnings in Deuteronomy 22, and believed that God would not have given such strong warning without purpose.) Robinson acknowledges that they (the clergy) were aware that these trends were not so much about changes in dress as they were symbolic of changes in sexual and political beliefs.

Historian James Laver explains that how a man dresses is symbolic of his relation to society and the way a woman dresses is symbolic of her relation to man. It seems that at the heart of the problem of androgyny (blurring distinctions between the sexes) is the rejection of the fact that God created the institution of the family as recorded in Genesis. Rather, androgyny finds its basis in evolution, believing that, as mankind slowly evolved, the patriarchal structure of society eventually came to be the acceptable social structural standard.

Laver goes on to explain that the complete emancipation of women means not only the disappearance of the family as we know it, but also of those religions that espouse the patriarchal order of society. He calls "pathetic" those "advanced" clergymen who think they can go on undermining the patriarchal system – which they equate with capitalism – and yet keep intact the patriarchal family. "These things stand – or fall – together." [80] The false ideas he was calling pathetic are indeed wholly feminist.

Note this warning by the Langner in 1959:

> The history of civilization has many examples of great nations which became effeminate and were destroyed by more virile but less civilized races which conquered and overran them. In all such effeminacy, clothes played a leading role . . . In conclusion, the invention of the trouser and the skirt has enabled Western men and women to achieve a balanced social and sexual relationship over the centuries which, if greatly disturbed, may produce some highly unexpected results."[81]

In Romans 1, we are told that ungodly and unrighteous people will exchange that which is natural for that which is unnatural. Obviously God-given gender would certainly have to rank as highly natural. The gender war is a war against nature, against creation and ultimately against the Creator.

I will long remember the day when I heard the speech. It was one of those impactful moments when one remembers exactly where he was. I was in our town at the intersection of Third and Main when I heard the chilling words from the leader of our nation, making an announcement during a White House party held for gays, with cheering in the background. They were celebrating a legislative victory in favor of their lifestyle. He boldly proclaimed that a new day had come and that folks who still hold onto old fashioned ideas are just going to have to get out of the way! The chills just came over me! In essence he was denouncing those of us who hold to a biblical standard. He has declared June as "National Gay Month." Is there any wonder that this same man refuses to hold the traditional celebration for the National Day of Prayer at the White House?

As we reach out to the unfortunate people in our society, we are seeing firsthand the devastation that comes from ignoring God's principles. As we work with these families, we can't help but contemplate the question, "Why is there such tragic dysfunction?" Young people today are trying to decide if they are going to be male or female. I have encountered some very interesting situations in our online clothing business, but the one that tops them all was the day "Michelle" called. In the deepest possible, truly authentic male voice, Michelle explained that "she" was the mother of three children, two boys and a girl. My curiosity got the better of me so I kindly asked her some questions about her growing-up days and her views of life. It then provided me with a springboard to share my testimony of why Jesus Christ is everything to me. We had an extended polite conversation but as I hung up the phone, I was just flabbergasted!

Another encounter involved a request for a skirt with ruffles. The measurements were unclear, so I made a phone call to find out what the lady's measurements were. The man who answered hemmed and hawed, finally admitting that the dress was for himself. Such bizarre scenarios are among the consequences of our society's departure from Bible-based roles. Ideas do have consequences, and our society is paying…and dearly!

Langner states that the return of beards has been an attempt on the part of some men to hold on to their feelings of masculinity as women have become more masculine in their dress. The clean shaving of men's heads may also be an attempt to hold onto a macho image in our androgynous society.

So Who Should Wear the Pants?

A frequent question is, "What is wrong with ladies wearing pants? Didn't men and women in the Bible both wear robes?" Please join me as we think together through these issues.

First, let me say that I admire the feminine cultural attire in the country of India. The ladies wear soft, beautiful in color, loose-fitting garments. For the most part they are both modest and very feminine. Included are long loose fitting trousers under long flowing tops, often with shawls. This has been their type of dress for many centuries. It is quite appropriate in my opinion. But since we are not in India, we'll deal with where we live.

My research on the origins of Western feminine pant wearing has impacted me profoundly and opened my eyes to the spirit that motivated its acceptance. This spirit which sought for power is still very alive in the bare-legged and tight-fitting pants of today. In addition to this, there are other reasons that women should not wear pants.

In biblical history men and women both wore robes. The primary distinctions involved style, trims, color and length. Generally, men's garments went to below the knee while women's went to the ankle or floor. Hair was an important part of gender distinction, longer for women, shorter for men. Also, there was the distinction of a man's body/facial hair as opposed to the smoother appearance of the female.

Granted, some ladies' trousers are more modest than short or form-fitting skirts. This is true –especially for loose "granny slacks" – but this would need to include being amply loose at the hip/derriere area. A question though: how many girls or young women do you know today who would be caught wearing granny slacks? Tight jeans are the style, and if blending in with society is the motivation for wearing pants, then granny slacks would be terribly uncool! Speaking of tight jeans, just when you thought that they could not get any tighter, they did! Now the denim comes woven with Lycra or Spandex so they can show every single curve and bulge. If that is not good enough, now you can just forget the jeans altogether – just wear leggings. That is flat-out sensual – no excuses!

Another problem with jeans is that they look inconsistent on a veiled woman. Somehow the two do not go together; they just don't fit. Even to the general populace, it looks like a contradiction. I want to say that kindly though, because some who have newly discovered the biblical teaching of the veiling might be in transition to a more complete understanding, and might not yet have considered Deuteronomy 22.

What about farming or sports? I grew up as an Iowa farm girl, driving tractors, milking cows, moving turkeys on range, doing pretty much everything that a farm girl could possibly do. I have been there, done that, *in a dress*. Below the knee, loose fitting skirt-like culottes at times would have been more modest and served better. Or there is the option of wearing pants or leggings under a dress when necessary. A dress or skirt should still cover the knees, even if leggings are worn. The principle of covering neck to knees is what applies here as well. Although leggings provide some covering, they are not a sufficient covering.

One complaint that former pant wearers sometimes have is that going to wearing skirts makes them feel vulnerable because they feel uncovered – it's hard to get used to the feeling of the movement of air around the legs. Again a practical solution could be leggings worn under the skirt or dress.

A very good reason for the wearing of skirts as opposed to pants is that, in our society today, skirts are an unequivocal statement of femininity. Pretty much anywhere you go, on any public gender distinctive restroom door, you will see the pictogram skirt symbol indicating the ladies room. It is still an unmistakably recognized feminine symbol in the western world. Of course, there are some transvestites who openly engage in cross-dressing, but even they are using skirts to make a feminine statement. While it is true that pants may no longer be seen by our society as a masculine statement, as they indeed were 50-60 years ago, the flipside is still true; skirts are, still today, clearly seen as a feminine statement. When people today mention unisex clothing, they are referring to the classic jeans and T-shirt. So when a girl wears a skirt, she is making a clear gender identity statement.

I have read reviews by men who would like to dress in skirts, high heels and other feminine apparel. There is a consistency to their logic; they don't understand why, if it's socially acceptable for a woman to wear men's attire, should men not be free as well to wear ladies' clothing? Rather than justifying what they desire, this might help us see a little more from God's perspective concerning women in pants.

With today's gender confusion and role reversals, wearing a skirt not only makes a statement to others around us of embracing our place in life, it also enhances our own feelings of femininity. This, in turn, impacts our conduct. Those in the fashion/designer world readily admit this. A friend of mine said that, when she used to wear pants, it made her feel more powerful. One woman acknowledged that after she began wearing skirts, she noticed that her attitude toward her husband began to change for the better. Another friend who made this change noticed that men started opening doors for her, treating her with respect.

I was contacted by a young student who is attending Castleton State College in Vermont. She is newly into skirt wearing. She shared with me her journey, which I then asked for her permission to share with you, to which she gladly consented. The following is her testimony:

> About wearing skirts; after a lot of thought and prayer, I have realized that it doesn't matter what society says about you or what you wear, but it is important to please the Lord in whatever you do. So I decided that wearing skirts and being the feminine beauty that God designed me to be would be a blessing, not only in my life, but would be a good example of modesty for all the girls around me who are growing up in a society of immoral values. The Bible says in Deuteronomy 22:5 "A woman shall not wear a man's garment, nor shall a man put on a woman's cloak, for whoever does these things is an abomination to the Lord your God." It's been a very interesting experience suddenly going from a tom-boy after 3 years of college and to enter my fourth wearing skirts, but I've had a lot of good feedback from people in and outside of the church. I feel in the months following my change to skirts and dresses that my personal goals have moved away from pleasing society and have moved towards God's will and a life of serving others. I am much happier now.

This beautiful young lady is expressing what I have heard so many women tell me in the past twenty years. And they are usually not coming from any kind of conservative background or being pressured in any way. I love her declaration of allegiance. That is really the bottom line in this whole modesty issue. Who are we living to promote, Christ or self? Are we willing and happy to identify with Him?

10

The Meaning and Scope of Modesty
Focusing on Inner Beauty

Modesty begins as a heart attitude, but it is also demonstrated by several visible aspects.

One such aspect is how modesty conducts itself. If you, as a lady, hug a man who is not your husband, avoid pressing yourself against his body. A light embrace is sufficient. There are ways of walking that can be provocative because they draw attention to the body; set up a full length mirror at the other side of a room and watch yourself walk toward it. Avoid strutting, which draws attention to the hips and bosom. Proverbs also has many warnings about flattering lips or wanton (promiscuous, flirting) eyes. Even if dressed modestly, we can still send immodest messages by our facial expressions. It is, no doubt, possible to flirt without saying a word. The light in the eyes speaks volumes. A wink of the eye may be as suggestive as a sheer skirt; or a flirting smile as alluring as a provocative pose. Modern media provides us with abundant examples of the haughty look and sensual gaze. Without a word, the tempting look says it all – "Come and get it . . ."

Modesty also involves our words. Avoid referring to bodily functions or body parts, especially in mixed company. Avoid words that can plant suggestive thoughts or visual images into men's minds, such as referring to yourself in the shower, etc. Don't talk about private, strictly ladies' issues in the presence of men; this is totally inappropriate! It's not their business and they shouldn't be hearing it. Also, a genuine compliment to a man is good, but a flirty one is not. Compliment actions and character, not looks and clothing. Caution in our speech is valuable because, as the old saying goes, "Words are like plucked feathers; once cast to the wind they cannot be recovered."

Our behavior does impact others, so use loving consideration. "Since men are visually stimulated so easily, dressing immodestly is a form of sexual harassment of men. Make it easier for them *not* to look."[82] Ladies, remember your male counterparts didn't ask for elevated levels of certain hormones; and God's design was not a blunder. His design was perfect and intended for mankind's highest good, but our sinful tendencies easily short-circuit God's best intentions for us.

A third visible aspect of modesty, our clothing, demonstrates either modesty or the lack of it. We will discuss details later, but any clothing that publicly displays body characteristics in an alluring way is wrong.

Just changing wardrobes, however, is not what God has in mind. In addition to dressing and acting modestly, He, first and foremost, desires that our will be totally yielded and surrendered to him. Out of this surrendered will comes a sanctified life.

> Sanctification, which literally means to be "set apart," is both positional and practical. Positionally, the believer is already set apart for God, and that is why all Christians are called "saints" in Scripture. "Saint" and "sanctification" and "holy" all come from the same root word. God has chosen us and set us apart for Himself. Yet, what is true positionally ought to be true practically. We ought to be set apart from sin and evil. And this practical or experiential sanctification applies not only to the soul, but also to the body.[83]

May we think of ourselves as being truly set apart to God – belonging to Him. Then, from our transformed, surrendered hearts will come modesty expressed outwardly.

Inner Beauty

I have had the privilege of watching several different potters at work. The making of a beautiful piece of pottery comes with first softening the clay and then applying just the right amount of pressure at the right times to create the desired shape. As I was watching a potter at work, the song "The Potter Knows the Clay" came to mind.

The Potter Knows the Clay

> I know you are going through the fire
> Its getting hard to stand the heat
> But even harder is the wondering
> Is God's hand still on me
> It's lonely in the flame
> When you're counting days of pain
>
> But the Potter knows the clay
> How much pressure it can take
> How many times around the wheel
> 'Til there's submission to His will
> He's planned a beautiful design
> But it'll take some fire and time
> It's gonna be okay
> 'Cause the Potter knows the clay
>
> Friend I just came through that fire
> Not too very long ago
> And looking back I can see why
> And that my God was in control

On the hottest day I'd cry
Oh Lord, isn't it about time

But the Potter knows the clay
How much pressure it can take
How many times around the wheel
'Til there's submission to His will
He's planned a beautiful design
But it'll take some fire and time
It's gonna be okay
'Cause the Potter knows the clay

He's planned a beautiful design
But it'll take some fire and time
It's gonna be okay
'Cause the Potter, He knows the clay[84]

The potter clearly knew what he was doing. He had in mind a beautiful design. It was functional pottery, so it needed to be made according to plan in order to fulfill the intended purpose. Even after being shaped, it would still take some fire and time in order to become useful. The pressure and heat were critical parts of the process.

You and I are clay in the hands of the Master Potter. He is fashioning us into beautiful, useful vessels that display the glory of his name. As we allow the Potter to apply pressure that sometimes brings pain, our clay stays soft and pliable. Hardening and resisting keep the design and beauty from taking form as He plans. We often have different ideas than the Potter as to the vessel's appearance or function, but genuine beauty and true usefulness come with trusting the hand of the Potter, believing that He knows best. He knows the clay; he knows just how much pressure we can take. At times we feel like we will break under the pressure; He understands that as well. God can even use broken pieces to form a beautiful mosaic, and often does. Sometimes what we think of as mistakes may actually be part of God's design to form a rare treasure. Especially for those ladies who have been wounded, I highly recommend a book by Dorcas Stutzman entitled *Trust or Control, Exposing the Root Cause of a Woman's Inability to Trust*.

God is also the Master Artist. He is painting a picture on the canvas of our lives. To the untrained eye, the brush strokes and colors of the Artist often don't make sense at the time. It can look as if He is making a mess of things, because we don't understand the beautiful final masterpiece that He has clearly in mind. God envisions His masterpiece, even when we can't understand what He is doing. We don't dictate technique to the Artist. It is all about trust, understanding that even things which we do not like are actually part of the process of creating beauty that brings Him glory. We can know joy when we trust what He is doing, and we will be amazed when we see the final masterpiece.

Our community has been shaken by the tragic death of a precious 18-year-old (and only) daughter of Laverne and Rebecca Miller. She was becoming quite a beautiful and accomplished young lady. It looked as though a very promising future ahead lay ahead of her, but God's ways are not our ways. She was snatched from this life in an instant as another driver collided with her vehicle at an intersection. She left behind many dear friends, as well as family, who are now deeply grieving the loss of her friendship while cherishing the memory of her extraordinary character. Although I am certain that the grief and pain made it difficult, Her best friend, Christine Miller, wrote a tribute to Anja and the true inner beauty she displayed as a daughter of the King. As her memories mixed with tears, she wrote the following:

Anja: A Life Reflecting the Beauty of Jesus

We stood with our arms around each other, our tears mingling, falling onto the freshly turned soil. It didn't seem right to see her name, followed by that final date "Anja Miller – 9-10-2013" on the wooden stake above the grave. After the accident that took Anja's life, we as close friends tried to remember just what it was that made her life so full of beauty.

It wasn't a beauty limited by Anja's sparkling blue eyes and strawberry blond hair. It was deeper, much deeper than skin. The light in her eyes came from her relationship with Jesus, and the confidence of who she was in Him. As one of Anja's best friends I knew her well enough to know she wasn't perfect, yet in the way she lived her life I saw a soul, beautiful because she chose, even when it wasn't easy, to follow the path to true joy – Jesus Christ.

On a mirror in her bedroom Anja posted two signs to remind her every day of the things that make one truly beautiful. The first one gave me a key to understanding just what it was that helped Anja to look beyond herself. It states, "Comparison is the thief of joy." The second sign reflects the purpose with which Anja lived her eighteen years on earth, "You are doing something great with your life – when you're doing all the small things with His Great love. – Ann Voskamp"

Anja understood the grace of God like few people I know, and as a result of this, she extended that grace to others. She had many friends, from lonely old women to peers in her youth group, who cherished her quiet words and compassionate listening ear. Everyone agreed that it was Anja's unassuming ways and quiet confidence that made her so comfortable to be with. Her sense of humor and ability to admit when she was wrong gave her a realness that all of us could relate to. But Anja's greatest gift to her friends was the way she lived out her relationship with Christ in a way that pointed us all to Him.

In the last several years of her life Anja learned the joy and contentment that comes through conscious thankfulness, counting one thousand gifts several times over. Anja loved creating beauty through the gifts God gave her. Whether expressing herself through music or art, Anja set about creating pieces that reflected the beauty she found in the world around her.

It was these values that gave Anja the kind of joy that gave her eyes such sparkle, and filled her laughter with bubbling happiness. And this happiness was genuine because it was based on her relationship with Jesus, not on her circumstances. Her beauty reflected the condition of her heart rather than the state of her hair. But this kind of beauty is evident only in a life completely transformed by the glorious grace and love of Jesus Christ. And it was this kind of beauty that Anja reflected as she trained her gaze on Jesus and gave her whole life to follow him to the end.

Albert W. T. Orsborn, an early Salvation Army General, captured our desire to also allow God to do His beautiful work in our lives with the words of the song "Let the beauty of Jesus be seen in me . . ."

A Christian woman, by her godly appearance, is an expression of the gospel of Jesus Christ. She mirrors Christ. She adorns the gospel, making it attractive to a dying culture. Her love for Christ is more compelling than fad or fashion. Let us be encouraged as princesses to live up to our calling as true daughters of the King. We live as those in a foreign country; our true home is Heaven. We have pledged our lives and our sacred honor to the King of Heaven. As His daughters, we who bear His name are the reflection of the glory of our King, our Father, whose image we bear.

True beauty is a life that shines forth the radiance of Christ, the indwelling Spirit of Jesus. A truly beautiful woman's cup is not full of self, it's full of Jesus. Her passion in life is to bring God glory, to honor Him. It is a Christ-centered and an other-serving life. A passion burns in her heart to know Christ and to make Him known, to influence those around her toward her Lord. He owns her, and she lives for the purpose of bringing Him glory. She is holy, set apart as His prized possession!

11

The Virtue and Effects of Modesty
Does Clothing Convey a Message?

Clothes do adorn the body, for better or for worse. They also give us distinction, individuality and honor. Were you to come upon a judge relaxing in a sauna, you would come to realize rather quickly that his dignity had stayed behind, high and dry on the shelf outside the door. His long black robes are what make him appear judicial and give him distinction. A policeman would not carry the same authority or respect of position were it not for his uniform. A pilot is respected in his cap and uniform.

Conversely, the lack of distinctive clothing is the great equalizer. The airline pilot and the ditch digger are indistinguishable if wearing the same outfit. It puts everyone on the level. This is why some schools, prisons, etc. require the wearing of uniform attire.

Research reveals that how a person dresses will affect his behavior. One case study revealed that, when school bullies were deprived of their rebel attire and given normal classic street wear, their behavior took a turn for the better. This principle is also used in the professional world. Image consultants are very aware of the fact that, as they help their clients to look nicer, the psychological benefits for the client are very positive, also. This, in turn, can even have physical health benefits.

Secular authors who study clothing agree that clothing is never just a frivolity. There is always meaning vested in clothes, whether or not the wearer understands that meaning. Clothing speaks. It lets people know our loyalties. To deny this is naïve at best. Yale graduate Gila Manolson was making the point to her class that our clothing reflects how we view ourselves. One bearded, pony-tailed, scruffily dressed student vehemently denied it and took serious issue with her. He maintained that clothing and appearance was a non-issue, *not* a reflection of how he viewed himself! So she asked him to come back to class the next day with a haircut, shaven and in a three piece suit. He fumbled, stammered and sheepishly had to concede the point. She believes that the defensiveness and even hostility encountered on the issue of modesty, is proof that people care *intensely* about the image they are projecting through their clothing.[85]

As God-honoring women, our attire should send the message that we are happy and accepting of our place in life as women. Women acknowledge that they feel more like ladies when they wear dresses. They also say that men treat them politely when they wear skirts. One woman told me, "Men open doors for me when I wear skirts, and they don't when I wear pants."

When I travel alone as a lady, it is interesting to observe how men seem to delight in being chivalrous. They enjoy doing things like opening doors for me and helping me with my luggage. In fact, some insist on it, and I observe that they are not necessarily extending the same offer to some other immodestly dressed women struggling with their luggage.

Recently in town, I was walking up the ramp to our post office with several packages in my arms. They were not particularly heavy – and I don't think I was showing any signs of being stressed – but a tall man stopped me and fairly insisted on carrying my packages and opening the doors for me. Even though I may not have needed his help, I gladly allowed him the honor of performing his masculine offer.

When we dress modestly, discreetly and in a ladylike way, there is a sense of strength and manhood that rises within the men around us. In our society, a man is inspired to respect and protect when he recognizes that a woman is comfortable with being female. Her femininity is a complement to his manly aspirations. Feminine clothing is certainly a part of conveying that message.

Clothing can also let people know where our allegiance is, spiritually speaking. Can they see our allegiance to our King? Or do we look like we are playing into the hands of the enemy? A young girl who had grown up as a non-Christian used to live an immoral life and dress provocatively. When she surrendered to Christ, the Lord totally changed her heart. The change was genuine, all the way to the outside. Later, at a public event, upon seeing some Anabaptist girls who were dressed provocatively, she observed, "Those girls do not realize what they are doing. I used to be 'in business,' but now I'm not." If you're not in business, don't advertise your assets.

Modesty Protects

J. Mark Horst, in a sermon entitled "Is Modesty Relative?" says:

> The purpose of modesty is to provide protection for both men and women from Satan's plan to twist God-given desires for his purposes. You ladies dignify yourselves through your modest appearance and demeanor. If you're married, your body belongs to your husband, and his body belongs to you. You are protecting that relationship. If you are unmarried, you put men on notice that your value as a person is because you are made in the image of God, not because you're able to attract a man. Your body is not for display to every curious onlooker.

It is reserved for the husband God will bring into your life, if He so chooses.[86]

If you want to attract a man of character, then dress like a woman of character so the right man can find you. If you want him to be your friend for life, the attraction needs to be more than physical. Immodest young women will attract attention from more men, but men will have more respect and honor for a woman who dresses attractively, but modestly. Men often have feelings of disrespect toward a woman who dresses immodestly in public. When a woman publicly presents herself as an exhibitionist, revealing her bodily charms, she is not seen by men for the real spirit/soul person that she is. Rather she is viewed as a *thing* – something to be ogled over, played with, used and then trashed. She is a *body*, not respected or loved for who she is. Her value is seen only in the wrapping. What's inside the box is not seen as significant or of value.

12

When Modesty is Missing
The Mystery of Sensuality

A. Tight clothing actually uncovers

Clothing can be made to conceal, or to reveal. Dannah Gresh says, "The allure of immodesty is not what is seen, but what is not seen."[87] Something that many women do not understand is that, when they wear tight-fitting clothes and reveal their figure, the shape of their body (even though covered with clothes) will draw a man's eyes and excite his passions as quickly and surely as will the sight of her actual skin. We have been told by men that, when clothing tempts their imagination, either by being tight or partially exposing skin, it is more provocative than if the woman were completely unclothed. When the eye sees an incomplete picture, the brain will automatically finish it out. A man's brain is especially good at this. The intrigue comes not so much in what is seen, but rather in the mental image he gets from finishing out the picture, even without trying. His imagination automatically kicks in; that's what tempts him. He's hardwired to be aroused physically by a visual image even before his brain can process the stimuli. The skimpy and tight fashions of today are more tempting to men than complete nudity would be. Surprising? Yes, but it's true. Total nudity would be somewhat anti-erotic or repulsive, but partial nudity is very alluring.

In the case of women's clothes, a little is worse than none, and it is spiritually devastating to men.

In *Changing Styles in Fashion*, Maggie Pexton Murray says, "Baring part of the body is, in most cases, infinitely more provocative than baring all of it, and the part that is bared constantly changes. Long skirts hiding the leg will give way to short skirts that flaunt them."[88]

In the imagination, the whole female body is a desirable object. Eroticism is kept alive by the changing of clothing fashions, which in turn emphasize, either by exposure or by semi-concealment, the different erogenous zones. A particular style in fashion may change or become even more revealing once it has exhausted its erotic appeal. This is the whole business of fashion.

Not playing fair

Women these days need to understand that dressing immodestly is not playing fair. Since a man can get into legal trouble for touching (or for making crude comments about) the parts of a woman's body that are considered by law to be "private" parts, wouldn't it be fair for women to treat them as private? According to the dictionary, private means "secluded from the sight, presence or intrusion of others; not available for public use, control or participation."[89]

Sight is to a man what touch is to a woman. Since inappropriate touching or comments are considered grounds for charges of sexual harassment of a woman, then a woman openly flaunting her body should be considered sexual harassment against men. Many immodest women have the flippant attitude of "Well, he just has to deal with it. This is just the world we live in!" Would these women appreciate it if the same was said about their response to unwanted touch? While this would not be a good approach, neither is it an appropriate attitude that men just need to get over it. When a man uses his muscles to overpower and take advantage of a woman's body, we call it rape. But what do we call it when a woman uses the power of her beauty to seduce a man? The high number of men behind bars for sexual misconduct is undoubtedly connected to the immodesty of women today. The exposure we see women parading today on the street would have landed them in prison in years gone by. There's something wrong here, and it's not fair.

A few years ago the Associated Press carried an article about a female reporter who entered the New York Jets locker room to interview one of the players while wearing very tightly fitting clothes. Some crude comments were made, raising a firestorm of public debate and controversy in social media. Typically, other women defended her right to wear whatever she wanted, without negative consequences. A representative for NOW (National Organization for Women) said that "…women are proud of their bodies," and charged that she should not be held accountable for what she was wearing because that would be "blaming the victim." One woman voiced her concern that asking this reporter to tone down her wardrobe would be embarking on a slippery slope which would lead to requiring women to wear burqas.

However, a male spokesman for the NFL said, "If you come into the NFL dressed the way that she is dressed, you are just asking for it." Obviously the female reporter didn't get it, as evidenced by another man's comment. "Listen, the woman complains about men ogling her… then she shows up on TV with cleavage from here to Halloween."

Meanwhile, one paralegal set the record straight. According to her analysis, the reporter needed to take responsibility for her clothing choices. She said, "I would not want a male reporter coming into the female locker room [half exposed]." (Now I apologize if this sounds a bit crass, but does not this illustrate precisely how inappropriate some women are today?)

Where has fairness gone? Many women obviously revel in the sense of the power they have over men through their sensuality!

Sensuality is beautiful, in the right place, at the right time, alone with your husband. Sensuality expressed outside of that setting in the view of another woman's husband becomes sinful; it is defrauding. It incites the passions of a man to desire or fantasize about that which is not his to have. Therefore, if it's not on the menu, keep it covered.

As an important side note, when your beauty *is* on the menu, then . . . let your hair down. Allow your husband to enjoy the beauty that was meant just for him. This *is* the right place; this is the right time. "God's intended purpose for you as a carefully crafted masterpiece is to 'intoxicate' one man with the fullest extent of your beauty."[90] The devil didn't invent erotic pleasure, God did. For more encouragement along those lines, I would recommend to you the book *Trim Healthy Mama* by authors Pearl P. Barrett and Serene C. Allison.

Regarding erotic body areas

I received a call one day from a Catholic lady from Ireland. She operates a girls' home, made up of street girls rescued from prostitution. She hoped to transform these girls into godly young women. Her intentions were good, but unfortunately her methods were not helpful. They involved cleaning up the distorted minds of these young ladies by flattening their chests and requiring them to wear completely plain and dark colors, devoid of any sense of beauty whatsoever. She wanted my help in this endeavor and was willing to pay me well. Some other questionable tactics increased my reservations and, after spending hours of phone time listening to her and trying to help her see alternative methods, I eventually had to tell her that I could not in good conscience be a contributor to this effort. We don't help young girls become lovely, feminine, gracious and godly ladies by denying who God made them to be. She was also missing some heart-soul issues central to godliness. Having shared this, I want to be clear that being made beautiful as a woman is truly a gift. Accepting our beauty is an important part of a healthy sense of womanhood; it is a special treasure for the *one* man in your life, not to be cheaply shared at random with every male.

We do not need to totally smother our femininity or deny the fact that we have curves, but if we dress in a way that clearly reveals the size and shape of our contours, then we are playing with fire. Although gravity dictates that garments will show the top side of our curves, when our clothing pulls in and hugs tightly to reveal the underside contours of these curves, it becomes inappropriate. If the garment is designed to make a focal point of the bust line or other curves, it is immodest.

The Methodist preacher and scholar Adam Clark, who lived in the early 18th century, taught that the private parts of the female body should be carefully concealed. He explained that the word "apparel" in 1 Timothy 2:9 is from the compound word, *katastole*. The stola was a Greek dress: a long piece of cloth which hung down to the feet in front and behind, girded with a belt. The katastole was an additional piece of cloth which hung down to the waist loosely over the stola. That extra layer of cloth around the upper body helped to provide proper modesty.[91]

B. Immodest attire is a stumbling block

A Christian lady should be especially conscious of properly concealing the erotic parts of her body that invite a man to lust. It is true that men ought not to be looking; however, it goes both ways. David's sin was in looking, but Bathsheba's sin was in showing. The reaping was a bitter dose of grief for both of them.

In Matthew 5:28, Jesus warned that "whoever looks at a woman to lust for her has already committed adultery with her in his heart."[92] Many women see the lust issue as simply *his* problem, not hers. It is true enough that if he lusts, it is a problem. The Apostle Paul says, however, that we should not use our liberty if we know it will be likely to tempt another to sin.

Lustful looking is a greater temptation for men, but feminine sensual dressing is the counterpart to the same sin. Jesus said that looking with lust is such a serious danger toward a destructive path that it would be better to have an eye removed than to continue down that path. If lust is so serious, is provoking lust not equally serious?

C. Provocative attire weakens marriage

The Beauty of Modesty states:

> Marriage is a divine institution of supreme importance to the welfare of mankind, and sexual immodesty is a temptation to married men to violate their marriage vows. It is an invitation to infidelity. It is not surprising, therefore, that as our society has become more sexually "liberated" – meaning more sensual and immodest – there has been a dramatic increase in adultery.[93]
>
> A woman who dresses in a sexually provocative manner may not be thinking of seduction or adultery at all. She may only want a little attention. In fact, she might be appalled at what some men "imagine"

when seeing her. If solicited for sex, she would probably reply with a slap in the face. Nevertheless, a woman must understand the language she is speaking to men. She must realize that if she dresses in a sensual way, she is unwittingly assaulting the integrity and security of marriage, because she is causing a man to look away from his wife and toward her. Many affairs have begun with a furtive glance.[94]

Jeff Pollard says it this way:

> At this point some sisters might object, "But I'm not trying to be sexy or tempting to men!" I trust this is the case. However, despite your best intentions, if you don a stretchy, skin-tight suit *designed* to play up your assets and then expose yourself to the gaze of men, you won't succeed in promoting chastity, no matter how hard you try. Actions speak louder than words; and in this case, Spandex speaks much louder than heart's desire. The same principle applies to short skirts, tight pants, and numerous other garments which expose and advertise the body rather than cover it.[95]

The Vaughans continue:

> In light of the value God places on marriage and fidelity, immodesty is no small sin. It is not simply a silly and vain form of self-display. It is a snare [that leads] to serious sin. And for those who are married, it is a provocation to commit adultery . . . A truly godly woman will do nothing to weaken marriage or strengthen lust. On the contrary, she rather will dress and behave modestly in order to preserve the sanctity of marriage, including her own.[96]

Proverbs speaks of the immoral woman, who spreads her charms abroad:

> And behold, there met him a woman with the attire of a harlot, and subtil of heart. (She is loud and stubborn; her feet abide not in her house: now is she without, now in the streets, and lieth in wait at every corner.)[97]

Today we see many a woman who, by her appearance, is not keeping within her marriage, her "house," what belongs only there.

D. Modesty attracts the right kind of man

A young woman desiring a husband will usually attract a certain kind of man based on her appearance. In other words, the bait determines the fish. Dress in such a way as to attract the kind of man you really want. If you seek a godly husband who will be committed to the Lord and to you for life, dress modestly. If you want one with lower standards and less commitment, dress otherwise. Your modesty lets a young man know you are not a cheap girl. If he wants to have you, he needs to pay the price of commitment and lasting love in order to win you. He is challenged to excellence in order to prove himself worthy of you.

As Dannah Gresh puts it in *The Secret Keeper*,

> Modesty protects the true secrets of your body for one man, requiring him to invest in your life in order to one day enjoy your allure. It invites a guy to earn your virtue. Finding love this way is a long and slow process, and it often seems like it will never happen. That's part of what makes it so sweet. Proverbs 13:19 says, "A longing fulfilled is sweet to the soul." It is the waiting that makes it so precious and that invites him to work to earn your heart.[98]

E. Immodesty demonstrates vanity

Immodesty is one expression of what is called vanity. Vanity, according to John Wesley, is "the love and desire of being admired and praised."[99]

The Vaughans explain vain conduct:

The world becomes their stage, and they aspire to be at the center . . . A vain woman really does believe that she is beautiful (whether she is or not). She is 'flaunting her stuff' precisely because she thinks she has it to flaunt. The turning heads stroke her pride. With each glance her ego swells . . . Why? Because vanity "forms the heart to such a profound indifference to the welfare of others, that . . . you will infallibly find the vain man is his own center. Attentive only to himself . . . he considers life as a stage on which he is performing a part, and mankind in no other light than spectators."[100]

While immodest, provocative attire has undesirable consequences, we, as daughters of the King, seek to follow a purer path. We desire the Lord's safekeeping over ourselves, the men around us and our future. Let's explore some practical ways to helpfully display our God-given femininity according to His wonderful design.

13

Practical Tips for Personal Modesty
Honoring God by Looking Your Best

There are unhealthy extremes of so-called modesty that would repress women into being less than God intended. In some societies, women are treated like mindless, unthinking and second-class persons, sometimes not allowed to show more than their eyes. Cultures that practice such things do not value women as equal in worth to men. Women are not allowed to show any femininity, beauty or creativity.

Those who are immersed in American culture may be tempted to, in reaction, equate biblical modesty with this cultural abuse of femininity. The cultural abuse of women, however, has nothing to do with the Bible, but is itself a reaction to the feminist spirit so prevalent in Western culture. If we carefully consider that the Bible invites us to view the entire topic from God's perspective, we can avoid both this extreme and the opposite ditch of embracing worldly fashion. Neither extreme is right.

Taking care of ourselves

As with many things in life, just because something is off course and wrong in one direction does not mean that it calls for swinging into the other ditch. Just because our world has such an extreme emphasis on external and cosmetic beauty does not mean that we as

Christians avoid looking in the mirror to give some attention to looking attractive. Do you remember, wives, how important it was to look good for the man you were courting? Just because he has now vowed and signed his name to be faithful to you "till death do us part" does not mean that he doesn't care how you look.

Shaunti Feldhahn, in her book *For Women Only,* asked men what is most important to them with respect to beauty. What do you think #1 was? It was that their wives would make the effort to take care of themselves, to look neat, fresh, clean, attractive and cheerful. Regardless of our size or physical features, this is something each of us can do. If your husband sees that you have no time or energy for trying to look your best, it makes it harder for him to maintain mental purity. You expect him to put great effort into guarding his mind from wrong images. Should you not work hard to be attractive in your appearance? Let's not get sloppy or careless just because he has promised faithfulness. You might think, "If he really loved me, why should it matter?" He does love you, but it still matters!

This concern was very high – top priority for most men, but it's extremely hard for them to tell their wives. This doesn't mean that we have to be cover models, or that we are failing if we are a size or two bigger than when we were married, but they want us to look good. They want it to be apparent that we care about how we look. After all, how you as his wife appear does reflect on the choice that he made. He still wants to be proud of that choice twenty years and six children later. We honor our husbands by looking our best. It is also true that we as women feel better about ourselves when we make the effort to look good. We also honor God by looking our best.

So, how can I look my best?

Let's consider several ways to take care of ourselves and look our best naturally, including taking care of our skin and using the colors we wear to bring out the best in terms of radiance and glow. Let's also look at ways we can use our clothing to bring proper proportion and balance to our faces and figures, so that, as people see us, the focus is more naturally drawn to the face. This is where we want people to focus. Your countenance reveals the heart of who you really are, and modesty will bring the focus to your countenance.

Skin – Two simple clues to healthy skin: drink plenty of water and wash your face in the morning and again at night. Use warm water first and then cold water. This opens your pores and keeps your skin smooth and clear. Good skin creams can be helpful, too. At some point, however, we do need to come to terms with our age and be at peace in the fact that, along with the benefits of age come wrinkles, and that is all right.

Allow me to say a word here about makeup. Certain Christian authors defend the use of makeup such as eye shadow, lipstick, etc. by mentioning different women in the Old Testament who used it, implying that Scripture endorses it. In reality, however, when the Bible comments that certain women were beautiful, it does *not* say that they used makeup of this sort. In Scripture the only woman named as using eye shadow and paint is Jezebel, not exactly a good role model.

Smile – Of course, the all-around winner for the best facelift a lady can have is FREE! Your lovely smile and a twinkle in the eye (not flirtatious, of course) can make you more attractive than any cosmetic assistance ever could. A cheery smile will beautify even the homeliest of faces. Even if you lack straight teeth, your sweet smile is a lot better than appearing unhappy.

Beauty as the world sees it is not the gold coin of human worth! Those with "perfect" faces are not more valuable than the less attractive ones. The world's misguided sense of human value is out of touch with God's perspective on beauty and your worth as a person whom He designed. We work with what God gave us, but we need to realize that our truest beauty comes with accepting graciously our features as given by a wise Creator. A proper focus allows us to spend our greatest energies attending to what God calls true beauty: a quiet and gentle spirit, yielded to His reign in our lives. It is truly as we yield to His plan day by day, that His spirit fills us and thus will spill out to others. They will see a mirror image of the Divine, a reflection of His beauty. This is, in God's eyes, "of great price," of immeasurable value. Our primary purpose for living is to glorify God, and that is not accomplished through a perfect face. Instead, His beauty is displayed through our sweetness and joy from having spent time in His presence, so that what shines out of us is the radiance of His light.

Dealing with body shapes

When God made people, he didn't use a cookie-cutter. We are each special – uniquely made. Our facial features and body shapes vary considerably, and we all have things about ourselves that we think are odd – we just do. That's okay; we can learn to be fine with that! Some of us are too big in the hips or too small in that department; too large busted – or too flat. Our neck is too short or wide, or perhaps too long and thin. Waist is . . . well, where is it? It used to be there. Relax – your value is not less without it.

Maybe you feel like a pear, or like a stick. The main thing you do not want is to accentuate your under- or over-sized feature, whatever it is. You don't want people's attention fixated on that part of you. With our overfed and underdressed culture, I think you probably know what I'm talking about. That is where clothing becomes your compassionate friend, and a full-length mirror your most honest companion.

With our clothing, we can create illusions that bring our little quirks into balance so that they are not as likely to become a focal point. These illusions can make you look taller (if you're short) or thinner (if you're heavy) or in other ways be helpful in bringing a healthy balance. It is possible to create lines that fool the eye.

Dressing with your style does not come with pursuing what is "in style." That is not a safe guide for you, anyway. When you find the particular styles that help you look good, you don't need to avoid using those styles frequently. If a particular style looks graceful and feminine on you, no one will think about it being your main style. On the other hand, if you dress in styles that don't look nice on you, it will be noticeable. It will likely take trial and error (sometimes, unfortunately, involving time and expense), but you can discover what looks good on you. Here are some helpful tips that might help you in the process.

Depending on the shape of your face, certain necklines will look better on you than others. How the hair and/or the neckline frames the face can help or hinder the beauty of the facial features God gave us.

Some faces seem downright gorgeous. They have perfect symmetry in the eyes and well-placed cheekbones; the nose is not too large or tipped in some odd direction. There are a few so blessed; if you are one of these, don't be proud. *You* didn't put yourself together – God did. He reminds us, "For who maketh thee to differ from another? and what hast thou that thou didst not receive? now if thou didst receive it, why dost thou glory, as if thou hadst not received it?"[101] However, if you are not put together in quite those ways but possess a few flaws, don't feel underprivileged; most of us can relate. You are still a beautiful creation, a tribute to the handiwork of God. We cannot change our physical features, but we can work on our characters and become women whose faces glow with sweetness and grace from the inside out.

This does not mean, however, that we pay no attention to the principles of order and design. As every good photographer knows, the positioning of people in a group will make or break the photo. If there is a good balance and flow, the picture looks great. It is also true on a personal level with our faces. How we position our variables will have a positive or a negative effect on how we appear. We accept our unchangeable features, but we work wisely with those things that can be positioned or changed.

Faces – Faces come in five basic shapes: oval, round, square, rectangular, or triangular. The way that you part and/or drape your hair will make a difference in enhancing or detracting from the symmetrical shape of your face. A good rule of thumb is to work toward an oval. Now, that does not mean a perfectly circular oval, outlined with hair, but it does mean to try to bring the balance of your face more toward a general oval appearance as opposed to square or round. With most shapes, side-parting the hair will serve best to help ovalize and soften the face. Center parts tend to make a face look long or square. Also cleaning up your eyebrows, especially excess growth between the brows, gives your face a clean, fresh appearance. If your facial features are extreme in some way, avoid necklines that copy the irregularity. For example, if you are square-jawed, don't wear square necklines. In general, if your face is too square or too round, use a contrasting neckline to bring balance.

Necks – For a short neck, an open collar or V-line helps. Avoid high collars or neckbands. You can minimize the appearance of a wide neck by bringing the neckline in close to the neck on both sides.

Shoulders – If your shoulders are too broad, avoid necklines that focus on the horizontal. Rather, try to create narrow vertical illusions. If shoulders are narrow or sloped, use a horizontal focus to your advantage, or lapels that point up and out. Shoulder seams can create effective illusions, so if you are narrow, keep the seams wider. If you are broad-shouldered, keep seams right on the shoulder bone, not beyond. A sewing machine can come in handy for making these little adjustments.

Arms – If your arms are too short, three-quarter length sleeves can be helpful in creating a look of length. If your upper arms are heavy – which tends to occur with age – avoid short or tight sleeves; these only accentuate the situation. Short sleeves on anyone are best one inch above or one inch below the bust line.

Bust – If you are especially large-busted, you already know the challenges you deal with, but these hints may help. Avoid any horizontal lines at the bust line, including sleeve length. Also, wear something that tapers in gently from the bust line toward the waist, slimming your midriff and helping to bring an illusion of proper proportion. Any belt needs to be kept small and non-contrasting.

Use lapels or open collars. Avoid plain and high necks, such as turtlenecks. Any vertical seams, small buttons or a vertically layered look help to create vertical lines. Never wear anything tight over your bust. A loose, open-front vest helps considerably, because it conceals and creates vertical lines at the same time. All this helps to minimize the bust line.

Waist – If you are fortunate to have a narrow waist, belts are okay. If you are wide in that area, however, I recommend not drawing attention to it with either wide or contrasting belts. Any belt will create a horizontal line. Again, using the layered look to create vertical lines is a good thing, especially if you are short. If you are short-waisted, wearing separates can bring a longer waist look by creating a longer visual on top. If you're long-waisted, wear a shorter top; this will create a shorter visual effect on top.

Hips, Bottom and Thighs – If you are horizontally challenged at these points, avoid excessive fullness in your skirt. However, you do need enough fullness for modesty's sake, including when you're sitting. Soft gathers or pleats may be helpful, but too much adds width. If your skirt is tight enough to hug the underside curve of the hip or thigh, it calls attention to the problem, and it's not pretty. Don't cinch yourself in too tightly at the waist; a gentle side taper is good.

If hips are too small, a gentle side flare helps to suggest what isn't there. Lots of women wear their weight on the thighs, but thankfully that is an easy problem to disguise. Too tight a fit makes the fact obvious, while proper ease camouflages it.

Another trick to divert attention from the width of your thighs is to bring the width of your shoulders out a bit, with slim shoulder pads or puffy sleeves creating a better balance. Wearing your skirts long and with a ruffle, flare, or other accents down low helps to divert the focus from your broad areas. When wearing any kind of separates, including sweaters and jackets, always avoid having the length of the top end at your widest point. Wear neutrals to de-emphasize your disproportionate features, such as a neutral skirt with your more striking colors on top to bring the focus away from your broad areas.

Short stature – If you are short and want to look taller, outfits of one color are helpful. Contrasting separates make you appear shorter. If you do wear separates, shorter jackets or vests draw the eye up, giving you more height. Try to create visual distance between your head and the floor by wearing your accents up high. Also avoid large prints, as they tend to overwhelm you. If short and heavy, you do well to think vertical. You can bring the illusion of being narrower by creating vertical lines with layering, like a darker jacket or vest, leaving the front open, over a lighter-colored dress.

Overweight – If overweight, here are a few slimming tricks using color. Keep one of your best colors close to your face to draw the eye away from your body. Avoid large prints, as they will increase your apparent size. With solid colored skirts, sewing very tiny vertical pin tucks into your skirt, approximately 5 to 6 inches each way from centerfold, can make you look 10 pounds lighter. (You can do this without opening the waistband or the hem.) You also do best to avoid anything tight or clingy, as this makes you look heavier and calls attention to the problem areas. Wearing lighter shades on your lower half makes you seem bigger; darker shades decrease size. Also use layering to create vertical contrast lines. It's best to keep your upper arms covered if you carry excess fat there.

Using your seasonal color palette to your advantage

Of course you can wear any color you want, but some colors just look a lot better on you than do others. The determining factors for what looks good on you has a lot to do with the inherited genetic code with which you were born. That code is what gave you your unique hair, skin and eye color. Wearing the colors that are right for you will bring out the best in the way God created you, making you feel beautiful; wearing the wrong colors will lessen your attractiveness. If you have been like me, your closet may be bulging because you thought certain colors or styles were nice, but you don't end up wearing them much. When you put them on, you really do not feel very attractive, so they just sit there taking up space. It is helpful to learn what your best colors and styles are, so you don't end up wasting time and money on the mistakes. You will know that certain things may look good on the hanger, but they are just not right for *you*. Don't even let them tempt you. This will simplify things by saving time, money and closet space. With only the right colors and styles in your wardrobe, you will have fewer clothes but more to wear.

A very helpful resource is *Color Me Beautiful* by Carole Jackson. She explains how your blend of skin, hair and eye colors will put you into one of the four different seasonal color palettes: Winter, Spring, Summer or Fall. Your hair and eye colors are dominant factors, but your skin's undertone is the primary factor that determines which seasonal palette is yours. At times as you tan or as your skin lightens with age, the best intensities for you may vary, but those colors will always be your best ones. Your seasonal palette will not change. Although your genetic code determines your seasonal palette, children in the same family may still vary a lot. My husband and I are both Winters, but among our four beautiful daughters, we have two Winters, one Autumn and one Summer.

If you don't know your particular season and don't have someone who understands and can help you, I would recommend getting Jackson's book. If you do know someone who understands, ask them if they would help you with finding your seasonal palette.

If you find frequent compliments coming your way in certain colors, that is a pretty big hint that those colors are in your seasonal palette. The truth is that most color seasons can wear most of the colors, but the shades or the intensities of the colors matter a lot if you want to look your best. The fact that all of this has to do with colors, shades and intensities makes it impossible for me to describe this adequately here, but I will try to help you with a basic understanding.

Determining your best colors

- If your skin, hair and eye colors have blue undertones, you are a Winter or a Summer.
- Winters are usually not blonde. Summers usually don't have very dark hair.
- If your skin, hair and eye colors have golden undertones, you are an Autumn or a Spring.
- Autumns are usually not blonde. Springs rarely have dark hair.

However, having stated these generalities about hair color, they do not always hold true.

In brief, Winters will look good in the vivid, intense, clear or icy colors that have blue undertones, while summers would wear the softer or muted shades of those same colors. So, for Winters or Summers, think cool.

Autumn colors are rich and vivid or muted with deep, warm, golden undertones, while Springs' best colors are the softer, always clear but more delicate, or brighter shades of those same colors. If you are an Autumn or Spring, think warm.

All the seasons need neutrals in their wardrobe:

- Winter's neutrals are cool tones, intense ones like white, black, navies and grays.
- Summer's neutrals are softer with cool blues, grays, eggshell and some browns.
- Autumn has golden warm neutrals in coffee browns, beige gold and bronze.
- Spring's neutrals run in the warm categories with lighter golden browns, beige, ivory, tan, gray or navy.

The neutrals will provide the base for your outfit, but your color splash is what will bring out the best in your face so it should drape close to the face.

Winters will usually look best in solids. They should avoid muted or subtle prints. When they do wear prints, especially next to the face, the print needs to have sharp contrasts – not necessarily large, but vivid.

Having mentioned these things, here is an encouragement to mothers: teaching your daughters the art of sewing is a truly valuable gift. Not only is it an important feminine skill to cultivate, but it is also easier to be modestly dressed if you know at least the basics of sewing and can do simple alterations and modifications. Sewing also opens up a whole world of creativity in design, giving you options not available in commercially made garments.

Things Modesty Avoids

To be practical, there are things that ought to be avoided if we want to dress with feminine beauty and Christian modesty. As we go along, I will at times mention a survey about modesty that was done by *The Rebelution 1 Timothy 4:12,* a teenage rebellion against low expectations. The survey was drawn from 1,000 Christian men and boys.[102]

Low or loose necklines – I want to put in a good word for the current neck scarf trend. It can do several positive things if worn correctly. Wearing the right colors next to your face serves to enhance your beauty and draws the focus to your countenance. It helps to provide coverage at the neckline and, if worn properly, may even provide extra layering over the bust line.

Tall men especially have difficulty when women's necklines are so low or loose that leaning forward even a little reveals far more than intended. Check yourself in front of the mirror. Lean forward a little and see whether your neckline is still concealing or not. And how low is too low? If a godly man's first thought upon seeing you is that he needs to be careful with his eyes, then too much is being revealed.

When you need to access something that is on a lower level, try squatting rather than bending. If you do need to bend, develop the habit of holding one hand to your upper chest to hold your neckline in, or try to turn the opposite way if you need to use both hands for what you are doing.

Eye traps – A skirt with accents or ruffles around the hem can be very feminine and acceptable if the skirt is long. But if it ends at the knee or above, it creates an eye trap at a less-than-modest place. In a man's eyes, a skirt with a slit is effectively no longer than the top of the slit. As for skirt length, as evidenced from the Greek word used for the cloaks that God made for Adam and Eve, you need to be covered *at least* from the neck to the knees. Skirts should always cover the knees when standing or sitting, including when the legs are crossed. Be careful to cross your legs modestly, making sure that the fabric drapes around to avoid a peep show.

Be careful about eye traps like lines in skirts that point toward an erogenous zone. If you do not want men to focus on your posterior, then it's best to not wear your glitter there, or other accents either for that matter. In the survey, guys were asked whether pants with writing across the back side was a problem or not. An overwhelming majority said it *definitely is* a problem! They said that it is like baiting for attention at that spot; it's asking guys to focus there.

Also avoid pointed waistbands, or other eye traps that point the focus to sensual body areas. Think carefully about where you want men to look. You may think it's just cute, but in the eyes of a man it says more. Again, ask yourself, "Where do I want the eye to focus?" The focal points you create will be what the eyes naturally follow.

The men surveyed were also asked if it is a problem for them if a dress is fitted at the waistline and worn with a waistband or belt. Very few had any problem with this at all. In fact, the guys saw it as being more feminine that way, but not immodest.

Short sleeves – How short is too short? They should be long enough or otherwise designed to prohibit a view of what is inside when the arms are in any raised position.

Short skirts – In the survey, the overwhelming majority said that skirts above the knees are a problem for them! When guys can see knees when a girl sits, it does present a challenge. Also, on the question of which is better, a knee length skirt, or an ankle length skirt with a knee high slit, they were almost equally divided, but many guys saw the knee length skirt as more modest. An overwhelming majority agreed that if the slit goes above the knee, it clearly is immodest! They felt that if a skirt is so tight that the slit has to be that high to walk in, then the skirt is too tight!

Tight skirts – Skirts should not be too tight around the hips. If tight enough to hug tightly below the hips, or if panty lines or indentations can be seen, the skirt is too tight; it is not modest. If fabric is too thin or hangs in a revealing way, you need a slip! A slip in a non-stretchy fabric will be far less revealing and much more modest.

The survey asked guys about the issue of being able to see the lines of undergarments through the clothing (for tops as well as the bottom half). By far most men were in agreement that it certainly is problematic.

Sheer clothing – Partially-seen skin is suggestive, teasing the imagination. According to Vaughan:

> Many blouses, sweaters and even dresses are designed to be sheer enough for the body or underwear to be seen. This is not an accident. It is by design . . . A woman who is bold enough to wear sheer clothing ought to be brave enough to discard it. For it is all the same to the male observer.[103]

"Sheer" and "revealing" are synonymous. If it can be seen through, it is not covered.

Sheer or thin skirts – The survey also addressed the issue of being able to see through a skirt when a girl stands where there is bright lighting behind her, such as in a doorway, entering a room from the outside. It is definitely a problem! If there is *any* question, do a light check. If in doubt, wear an extra slip (no lady is fully dressed without a slip)! This is a situation, however, that can happen totally unintentionally in the scramble to get dressed and out the door in a hurry. I am probably not the only one who has discovered, to my horror once I'm too far from home, that in my haste I left without a slip. If that happens to you, find a different doorway or try to slip in very close behind someone else to avoid the light shining through from behind. Of course, if you are wearing a light colored skirt, maybe it is a good time to ask someone to bring you a good book, and you can just stay in the car or turn around and go back home. Better yet, keep a spare half-slip stashed somewhere in your vehicle.

Baby bumps – I know they're cute, and I'm sure that, to your husband, your little bump is precious! But please, dear, do you need to be showing all the men around you the underside of your pregnant belly? Is that appropriate? It is really not their business, and I know for a fact that a lot of them would rather not have to see it. Isn't it sort of like publicizing and putting a big exclamation mark on a sexual statement? After all, baby bumps don't come from eating too many cookies. You have a baby bump because of your sexuality. Of course I understand well that the last month or two you may feel anything but sexy! But as long as this bump is attached to your body, please my friend, treat it with as much privacy as possible. The principle of concealing the underside of our curves for modesty's sake applies here. In my mother's day, an expectant mom stayed home from church the last few weeks for discretion's sake – which I'm not suggesting that at all – but we do seem to have "come a long way, baby," haven't we?

Tight Clothing – Avoid even semi-tight T-shirts, turtlenecks, knits – or anything that is worn too snugly. Perhaps it doesn't look too tight if you stand in front of the mirror and pull it forward, but as soon as you move around, it stretches tight around the bust and reveals the underside of the breasts. In the survey, men also noted a problem when a woman wears a button-down shirt or jacket left open, with a tight shirt underneath. Many guys felt that, if it is obvious that the shirt is tight underneath across the bust line, then it really does little good to wear a loose shirt or jacket on top.

A good rule to go by is "Long, Loose and Lovely." A lady should almost always have two layers over her chest area. A camisole is a great idea. It helps at the same time to solve the see-through problem and to disguise the clear outline of the bust and/or undergarment straps in the way the fabric drapes. Please, especially when wearing a T-shirt, *always* have another layer either underneath or over top. Oftentimes the style being worn is not what is offensive, but simply the fact that it is being worn too tightly. A larger size can solve this problem. If you have a too-tight shirt, this is a great opportunity to bless a friend who is smaller on top. Also, a reality about being overweight is that stuffing ourselves into something that is too small does not help us look thinner, it only emphasizes the obvious fact.

Designs that draw attention to the bust – Some dresses, blouses or shirts are designed to draw attention to the bust. These create a visual magnet: an empire waist with gathers, and a bow, loop, or something drawn up between the breasts. What these actually are saying is, "Hey, everybody, would you please look here!" Protect yourself, because there are plenty of the type of men around town who will be glad to look. You do not want to know what they are thinking!

Also be careful about words written across the chest, especially if worn tightly. Words are meant to be read; to read them, men need to look. Be careful about what you advertise.

Don't show your underwear – Wearing clothing on the outside that resembles underwear is also suggestive. Beware of any body position that exposes any part of your undergarments, including straps, etc. When a guy sees part of your underwear, his mind can quickly imagine you in only your underwear.

About now you may be thinking, "Oh help us all! Why does all this matter? Can't guys get a grip?" It would help girls a lot in understanding a young man's perspective if they could live just one day – or even one hour, for that matter – inside a young man's head. Can't he just control his thoughts, or look the other way? Yes, he should; yes, he can, and many will; but if you are truly a Christ-reflector, he should not need to avoid you.

The guys surveyed were overwhelmingly together on this issue of ladies' or girls' underwear or straps showing. This question brought the greatest unified response of all the questions asked. It is an absolute "no, no" – definitely not helpful!

Underwear-type clothing – While I was driving in a large city one day I was somewhat taken aback to see a woman jogging along on the sidewalk past a large hospital complex in only her bra and panties . . . white ones at that. Now wait a minute; did I state that correctly? Sounds impossible! Unfortunately, it's the truth. It struck me then that about the only difference between underwear and outerwear these days is that, if white, it is seen as underwear; but if colored, it is considered outerwear. But then, underwear is colored, too. You know, it really gets confusing! It used to be that a slip was worn *under* a dress, but now it is also worn outside – sometimes over a T-shirt. Oh, but if colored or patterned with floral print, then it's not a slip, so I guess it is acceptable . . . Really? . . . Is that right? Same thing with tank tops. Seriously, ask the men around you how it strikes them, especially if worn over a white T-shirt (but be aware that some enjoy seeing you dress like this, although for the wrong reasons). If fashioned like underwear, please practice the "under" part in underwear. Remember the power of suggestion.

Bare midriff – At no time should bare skin show between your skirt and blouse. Girls, be very careful about this, especially when playing vigorous sports or bending over. If your blouse is too short and your skirt is too low, then please wear a full slip. Our society has fallen off the deep end here. One day while at Burger King, I was stunned to observe the "bare fact" that we need to shield our sons not only from the cleavage in front, but now also from serious cleavage behind. How much more pathetically inappropriate can it get?!

Consider the intent – Why, at a wedding, is the groom dressed with multiple layers right up to the throat, while his bride stands beside him quite exposed on top? Ditto for the bridesmaids and groomsmen. What is going on here? And, when you see a guy and gal walking along, why are the guys almost always the ones wearing the longer and looser shorts, while the girls are wearing extremely short and tight shorts? If the men are the ones that especially struggle with lust, why should women exacerbate the problem by wearing clothing so much tighter, and with so much more skin showing? Instead of asking, "What's wrong with this or that?" let's double our efforts to make sure our clothing is not cause for stumbling for our brothers in Christ.

Just imagine the average guy from 100 years ago, catapulted into the streets of 2014. Things have changed dramatically!! (Have you seen *Time Changers*?) If you check out pictures of what was worn as underwear 100 years ago, you can see how it obviously provided better coverage and modesty than today's normal street wear. Now the good side of this is that a godly young lady today, dressed attractively, yet modestly, is blessed to have a greater opportunity than ever before to be a shining reflection of Jesus in our morally dark world. One look at her reveals that she belongs to the King!

Having considered these things, may we prayerfully evaluate our wardrobes in the light of these guiding principles. Ask God what He would have you do. If married, ask your husband. If unmarried, ask your father. Or ask a trusted godly friend. Are there any changes God may be asking you to make? Are you willing to make those changes for the sake of your brothers in Christ and for the sake of your witness as a daughter of the King?

How Attractively May I Dress?   Is Adornment Wrong?

We don't understand the Word of God as condemning all adornment. When the apostle Paul instructs women to adorn themselves in modest apparel, he recognizes that clothing is aesthetic. Clothing can add to the loveliness of femininity, as the word *modesty* would indicate. *Modest* means, "neither bold nor self-assertive;

unpretentious," [104] "decent, well-ordered." [105] The idea would be "nice, but not over-done" as opposed to self-conceit or vanity.

Modesty also includes being neat and orderly. Therefore, sloppiness and untidiness do not lend themselves to modesty.

So now the question: what is over-doing it? What is ostentatious? A good gauge would be to check your motives: why do you seek to dress beautifully and attractively? Embracing your femininity is healthy and good; enhancing your sensuality for the public is not. Boldness that screams "Look at me!" is also opposed to the humble heart that is modest.

> True Christian humility . . . seeks neither place nor praise. It is opposed to the pride and vanity displayed in immodesty. It is surely no coincidence that the very word *modest* may also be defined as "humility" or "reticence." It is the reluctance to advance oneself, to put oneself on display, or to promote oneself.[106]

Conclusion
Encouragement to Christ-Followers

One factor that can be a stumbling block in our churches is that of reacting to our past. It is dangerously easy to live life in reactionary mode. We become so focused on avoiding certain errors that we do not realize that we are being blindsided by a different kind of wrong. Let's not allow our distaste or disdain for past abuses or errors in our church experience to cause us to reject the things that *were* good and helpful, even if some were improperly emphasized. Christian discipleship calls for a surrender to all of Scripture, even to those things we feel are besmirched by over-emphasis, heavy-handedness, hypocrisy, or even by misunderstandings of Scripture. Embracing an opposite error does not correct past wrongs or lead us on the path of faithfulness. Let's take a careful, honest look at Scripture for what it is and commit ourselves to living obediently.

In the matter of modesty, let's not assume, just because we have not listed a specific rule about certain things, that the door is wide open to anything not spelled out. Our church conference intentionally does not spell out a long list of rules regarding our appearance, and that is certainly not our intention here. We do believe, however, that when genuine Bible principles are carefully taught, we will be able, by the aid of the Spirit, to apply these truths to our lives in a variety of ways.

Truth has many right applications. One need only consider creation to see that God loves tremendous creativity and diversity. As persons made in His image, we also enjoy and appreciate good, healthy things in many different ways. Creativity in dress is certainly one of these ways. While enjoying our God-given creativity, we do so with a determination to honor, obey and delight Him in the process. We need to be settled in our minds about which lines we will not cross.

The really wonderful fact is that, as children of the King, we have a lot more allowance for creativity than do our culturally-molded counterparts! They are limited to the current fashions of the day. They would not be caught dead in something that was considered beautiful ten years ago, or even three years ago. They lack freedom to dress in a way that is beautifully feminine if the current trends don't allow it. Their only option is to yield to what current fashion dictates, as though fashion were God. This commitment to the god of fashion is actually a sort of unwitting, willing bondage. To be "cool" and accepted by peers, they do not have any other option than to conform. They make the declaration that, "Nobody's gonna tell me what I can or can't wear!" while at the very same time they are letting the world tell them what they *must* wear. It is a bondage which they are willing to pay huge sums of money to serve. And to what purpose? The approval of peers? But the princess lives for the smile and approval of her King.

The truth is, we all have a dress code. Either we have thought through our choices and made our own decisions, or we have let other people do our thinking for us and have automatically accepted their conclusions. We need to guard against the snare of desiring popularity. Many compromises of one's conscience come as a result of the desire for popularity. We tolerate and indulge in things that we know are not best just to follow the "cool" folks. Please dear sister, don't sacrifice your worth on the altar of popularity. God wants your heart. He asks for your obedience and allegiance above other voices that call you.

God's Word says that we are not to love the world or the things of the world. "The fashion industry caters to pride, the lust of the flesh, and the lust of the eyes, not purity and holiness. Its purpose is not *covering* the body; but sensually *packaging* or *uncovering* it."[107] The world is open about its carnal intentions. What is strange is how Christians try to justify or deny the intentions of the very things that the world calls sensual. The world doesn't care about what God thinks, so they are straightforward about the intentions in the designs that they wear. In their eyes, a little sin and a little lust is okay! It's to be expected – just don't let it get out of hand. They scoff at purity and a holy standard. As Christians, we know we should care about what God thinks, but acceptance by the world sometimes means too much to us. We are tempted to compromise by persuading ourselves that light shades of gray are really okay. Consider our forbearers who literally lost their lives rather than compromise obedience to Christian principle.

> The world and its gods of fashion must not be the standard for how Christians dress . . . One noted fashion historian writes, "All my research has led me to believe that the concept of beauty is sexual in origin, and the changing ideal of beauty apparently reflects shifting attitudes toward sexual expression." . . . Regarding feminine beauty the Holy Spirit declares by Solomon, "Favour *is* deceitful, and beauty *is* vain: *but* a woman *that* feareth the LORD, she shall be praised." *This* is the standard.[108]

Whether we realize it or not, clothes are a language with which we communicate to others.

Christian modesty is governed by a proper understanding of who we are in relation to God. We understand that we are to be reflections of Him instead of advertising ourselves.

Pray for your pastors and encourage them in their teaching on this very difficult topic. Many things the pastor admonishes from the pulpit are matters of the heart, not things that are obvious to the eye. Pastors find that teaching the biblical application of modesty is very hard to do because they don't want to offend ladies. Too many times the very offenses being addressed are in plain sight. It takes a tremendous amount of wisdom and courage to avoid offending those for whom the teaching is most applicable. Then, as the Vaughans put it:

> The leadership must be willing to speak in love to anyone who continues to "strut their stuff". . . We would add that one of the most powerful forms of instruction is example. Therefore, the leadership of any church must evaluate its own example in the area of modesty. Men and women on a church staff must realize that they are an example in every area of their lives. This includes how they dress . . . If the pastors' or deacons' wives are dressed attractively yet modestly, then they will set a powerful example for the rest of the women in the church. For the most part, the "culture" of a local church will reflect the priorities and patterns set by the teaching and example of the leadership. The virtues of the leaders become those of the church.[109]

In conclusion, as stated by J. Mark Horst:

> We could say then that the over-arching reason for modesty is to allow men and women to fulfill God's purpose for them individually and collectively as the church. Modesty removes unnecessary distractions

from the public assembly, allowing worshipers to focus on God, not on exposed flesh or on behavior that attracts attention to one's self. In our interaction with the world, modesty gives evidence of our commitment to God and the principles of His Word. It gives protection from exploitation and demonstrates our understanding that our bodies are the dwelling place of the Holy Spirit. Modesty enables our witness in a positive way.[110]

For those who would be helped by connecting with the author, Evelyn may be reached at: biblicalfemininebeauty@gmail.com

Bibliography

NOTE: We recommend caution with regard to some of the resources consulted in the writing of this book.

American Word Origins "teenager" on Answers.com. *America in So Many Words* Copyright © 1997 by Houghton Mifflin Company. Published by Houghton Mifflin Company.

Anonymous, *The Sin of Bathsheba, An Appeal to Christian Women by a Brother in Christ*, a gospel tract.

Clarke, Adam and Earle, Ralph, *Adam Clarke's Commentary on the Bible*, Kansas City, MO, Beacon Hill Press of Kansas City, 1967

Cunnington, C. Willet and Phillis, *The History of Underclothes*, New York, NY, Dover Publications: 1992

DeMoss, Nancy Leigh, *Modesty, Does God Really Care What I Wear?*, a CD.

Feldhahn, Shaunti, *For Women Only*, Colorado Springs, CO, Multnomah Books: 2013

Gresh, Dannah, *Secret Keeper, The Delicate Power of Modesty*, Chicago, IL, Moody Publishers: 2005

Horst, J. Mark, Sermon notes: "Is Modesty Relative?"

Jackson, Carole, *Color Me Beautiful*, New York, NY, Ballantine Books: 1987

Kassian, Mary, *The Feminist Mistake, The Radical Impact of Feminism on Church and Culture*, Wheaton, IL, Crossway: 2005

Langner, Lawrence, *The Importance of Wearing Clothes,* Los Angeles: Elysium Growth Press, 1991. [NOTE: This resource <u>not</u> recommended]

Laver, James, *Modesty in Dress, An Inquiry into the Fundamentals of Fashion*, Boston: Houghton Mifflin, 1969.

Manolson, Gina, "You Are What You Wear", Nov. 16, 2009 post, https://jewishkitty.wordpress.com/2009/11/16/you-are-what-you-wear-by-gila-manolson/

Murray, Andrew, *Humility*, Grand Rapids, MI, Bethany House Publishers: 2001

Murray, Maggie Pexton, *Changing Styles in Fashion: Who, What, Why*, New York, NY, Fairchild Publications: 1989

Myer, Carolyn, *Know Why You Are Veiled*, Elm, PA, Executive Printing: 2010.

Pollard, Jeff, *Christian Modesty and the Public Undressing of America*, San Antonio, TX: The Vision Forum, 2003

Schrock, Simon, *The FCM Informer*, "Please Sisters", Fellowship of Concerned Mennonites, publishing date unknown

Shank, Tom, ed., *Let Her Be Veiled*, 3rd Edition, Torch Publications: 1992

Smeal, Robert, ed., "Thoughts on Dress," *The British Friend*, Vol. XXXV (10th month 1st, 1877)

Smith, Catherine and Greig, Cynthia, *Women in Pants, Manly Maidens, Cowgirls, and other Renegades,* New York, NY, Harry N. Abrams, Inc., 2003

Students of the Advanced Training Institute International, *How to Conquer the Addiction of Rock Music*, Oak Brooke, IL, Institute in Basic Life Principles: 1993

Stutzman, Steve, *Let Her Be Covered,* a CD, 2010

The American Heritage Dictionary, 2nd College Edition, Houghton Mifflin Company, 1982. Print.

The Holy Bible, English Standard Version, copyright 2001, by Crossway Bibles, a publishing ministry of Good News Publishers.

The Holy Bible, King James Version.

The Holy Bible, New King James Version, copyright 1982, by Thomas Nelson, Inc., Nashville, TN.

The Perrys, "The Potter Knows the Clay," http://www.lyrics.com/potter-knows-the-clay-lyrics-the-perrys.html#jy98kpPAwQbiYjou.99. May 27, 2016

The Rebelution 1 Timothy 4:12, "The Modesty Survey Results", http://therebelution.com/blog/2007/02/the-modesty-survey-results/

Vaughan, David and Diane, *The Beauty of Modesty,* Nashville: Cumberland House, 2005.

Webster's New Collegiate Dictionary. Springfield, Mass: G. & C. Merriam Co, 1981. Print.

Vines Expository Dictionary of New Testament Words. Old Tappan, NJ: Fleming H. Revell Company, 1966. Print.

Wikipedia.org, "1945 – 1960 in Western Fashion", May 24, 2016, https://en.wikipedia.org/wiki/1945%E2%80%931960_in_Western_fashion

Wikipedia, "1970s in Western Fashion", May 17, 2016, https://en.wikipedia.org/wiki/1970s_in_Western_fashion

Yoder, Val, "Holiness for Dummies," *The Monitor*, March, 2014.

Endnotes:

1. Pollard, Jeff, *Christian Modesty and the Public Undressing of America*, 15.

2. Romans 3:18.

3. John Whitehead, *The End of Man*, p. 31, as quoted by Vaughan, David and Diane, *The Beauty of Modesty*, 40.

4. Sproul, R.C., *Life Views*, 126, as quoted by Vaughan, 40.

5. Matthew 5:13-16, NKJV. (NKJV signifies scripture taken from the New King James Version. Copyright ©1982 by Thomas Nelson, Inc. Used by permission. All rights reserved.)

6. Vaughan, David and Diane, *The Beauty of Modesty*, 45.

7. Barna, George, "Survey Shows Faith Impacts Some Behaviors but Not Others," *The Barna Update* (barna.org), Oct. 22, 2002; as related in Vaughan, 41.

8. Tozer, A.W., *The Knowledge of the Holy*, 6-7, as quoted in Vaughan, 153.

9. Vaughan, 31.

10. Romans 12:2.

11. Genesis 1:31.

12. Genesis 3:7,10,21. Parenthetical comment inserted by author.

13. From The Holy Bible, English Standard Version, copyright 2001, by Crossway Bibles, a publishing ministry of Good News Publishers. Used by permission. All rights reserved.

14. Laver, James, *Modesty in Dress*, 40.

15. see Shank, Tom, *Let Her Be Veiled*, 77.

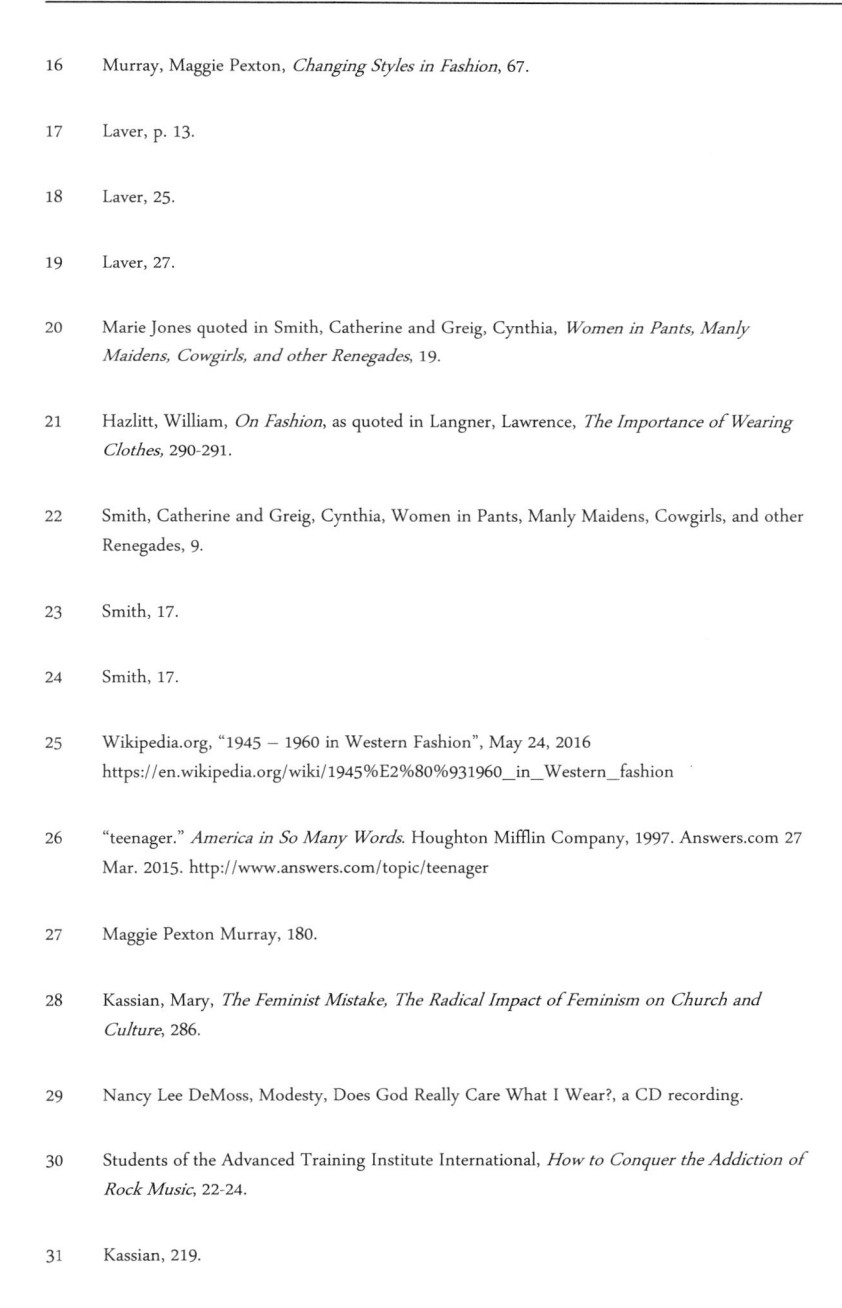

16   Murray, Maggie Pexton, *Changing Styles in Fashion*, 67.

17   Laver, p. 13.

18   Laver, 25.

19   Laver, 27.

20   Marie Jones quoted in Smith, Catherine and Greig, Cynthia, *Women in Pants, Manly Maidens, Cowgirls, and other Renegades*, 19.

21   Hazlitt, William, *On Fashion*, as quoted in Langner, Lawrence, *The Importance of Wearing Clothes,* 290-291.

22   Smith, Catherine and Greig, Cynthia, Women in Pants, Manly Maidens, Cowgirls, and other Renegades, 9.

23   Smith, 17.

24   Smith, 17.

25   Wikipedia.org, "1945 – 1960 in Western Fashion", May 24, 2016 https://en.wikipedia.org/wiki/1945%E2%80%931960_in_Western_fashion

26   "teenager." *America in So Many Words*. Houghton Mifflin Company, 1997. Answers.com 27 Mar. 2015. http://www.answers.com/topic/teenager

27   Maggie Pexton Murray, 180.

28   Kassian, Mary, *The Feminist Mistake, The Radical Impact of Feminism on Church and Culture*, 286.

29   Nancy Lee DeMoss, Modesty, Does God Really Care What I Wear?, a CD recording.

30   Students of the Advanced Training Institute International, *How to Conquer the Addiction of Rock Music,* 22-24.

31   Kassian, 219.

32   Kassian, 190.

33   Romans 1:18-19, 21-22, 25-26.

34   Adler, Margaret, *Drawing Down the Moon*, 1986, 182; as quoted in Kassian, 241.

35   Kassian, 277.

36   Pollard, 37-38.

37   Pollard, 42.

38   Pollard, 42.

39   Lencek, Lena, and Bosker, Gideon, *Making Waves: Swimsuits and the Public Undressing of America*, 51, as quoted in Pollard, 44-45.

40   Ibid.

41   Ibid.

42   Lencek and Bosker, 76, as quoted in Pollard, 45.

43   Pollard, 43.

44   Langner, Lawrence, *The Importance of Wearing Clothes*, p. 43.

45   Pollard, 44.

46   Pollard, 43-44.

47   Pollard, 47.

48   Vaughan, 175-176.

49   Vaughan, 171.

50   Vaughan, 172.

51 Luke 14:33, NKJV.

52 Vaughan, 184.

53 Vaughan, 168.

54 John 14:15.

55 Val Yoder, "Holiness for Dummies," *The Monitor*, March, 2014, 1.

56 1 Corinthians 6:19-20, NKJV.

57 Vaughan, 64-65, including Sherman's quote found in Charnock, *The Existence and Attributes of God, Vol. 1*, 220.

58 Vaughan, 55-56.

59 Pollard, 72.

60 Romans 14:15, NKJV.

61 Vaughan, 164-165.

62 1 John 4:20b.

63 Ephesians 4:15.

64 Hebrews 10:24, NKJV.

65 Vaughan, 165.

66 Horst, J. Mark sermon: "Is Modesty Relative?"

67 Anonymous, The Sin of Bathsheba, An Appeal to Christian Women by a Brother in Christ, (a gospel tract).

68 Vaughan, 162.

69 Pollard, 65.

70   Murray, Andrew, *Humility*, 83, 84, 63.

71   Deuteronomy 7:9.

72   Carolyn Myer, *Know Why You Are Veiled*, 30.

73   Steve Stutzman, *Let Her Be Covered*, 2010, a CD: This paragraph is not an exact quote, but my retelling of Steve's story.

74   Romans 3:4.

75   Daniel 1:8.

76   II Timothy 2:12b.

77   II Chronicles 16:9a.

78   DeMoss, Nancy Leigh, Modesty, Does God Really Care What I Wear?, a CD.

79   Langner, 333.

80   Laver, 178.

81   Langner, 67, 70.

82   Vaughan, 106.

83   Vaughan, 166-167.

84   The Perrys, "The Potter Knows the Clay," http://www.lyrics.com/potter-knows-the-clay-lyrics-the-perrys.html#jy98kpPAwQbiYjou.99. May 27, 2016

85   Manolson, Gina, "You Are What You Wear", Nov. 16, 2009 post, https://jewishkitty.wordpress.com/2009/11/16/you-are-what-you-wear-by-gila-manolson/

86   Horst, "Is Modesty Relative?"

87   Dannah Gresh, *Secret Keeper*, 61.

88   Murray, Maggie Pexton, 13.

89   "Private." *The American Heritage Dictionary*, 2nd College Edition, 1991. Print.

90   Dannah Gresh, *Secret Keeper*, 83.

91   Schrock, Simon, *The FCM Informer*, "Please Sisters!"

92   Holy Bible, NKJV.

93   Vaughan, 79.

94   Vaughan, 80.

95   Pollard, 68.

96   Vaughan, 80.

97   Proverbs 7:10-12.

98   Dannah Gresh, *Secret Keeper,* 57.

99   Smeal, Robert, ed., "Thoughts on Dress," The *British Friend,* Vol. XXXV (10th month 1st, 1877): 276

100   Vaughan, 113. Quotation from Hall, *Works*, 1:35.

101   1 Corinthians 4:7.

102   The Rebelution 1 Timothy 4:12, "The Modesty Survey Results", http://therebelution.com/blog/2007/02/the-modesty-survey-results/

103   Vaughan, 92.

104   "Modest." *Webster's New Collegiate Dictionary*. Springfield, Mass: G. & C. Merriam Co, 1981. Print.

105   "Modest." *Vines Expository Dictionary of New Testament Words*. Old Tappan, NJ: Fleming H. Revell Company, 1966. Print.

106 Vaughan, 183.

107 Pollard, 65.

108 Pollard, 68. Quotation from Valerie Steele, Fashion and Eroticism: Ideals of Feminine Beauty From the Victorian Era to the Jazz Age.

109 Vaughan, 165-166.

110 Horst, "Is Modesty Relative?"